My Life

My Military Memories

My thoughts

My way

I was born January 15, 1967
In North Adams Massachusetts
In the words of my late Father
" what You see is what You get "

Alan Haskell SR

ISBN: 978-1-958150-85-6

Published - December 2025
To contact author
https://www.facebook.com/alan.haskell.2025

# Preface

All who read this book or collection of a lifetime of memories and lessons learned must in my viewpoint understand that All Americans are free only because of the sacrifices of those who died, got wounded or served this nation. This is from George Washington to present day and beyond. Many photos and documents are going to be presented so I can share a portion of my life with everyone who sees and reads them.

My mindset in many ways has never left the Army life so to speak even 30 plus years Later. I do believe the old saying that you can take the soldier out of the Army but can't take the Army out of the Soldier or at least in my case!! This applies to all branches of the armed services. I also believe that all who have served are forever changed and have some form of PTSD or other mental/emotional hang ups including myself. My Issues have been ~~under~~ under control but at times rear their ugly head when you least need them.

At times I believe I have hurt peoples feelings with my no nonsense military type of attitude and sternness. My practically fearless mindset can be a good thing or cause big Issues for others especially for those I love the most in this life!

1

# Intro

This book as you can see is hand printed. I do understand that this is not normal for a modern book. this idea has come from several sources in my life including my father and Steve my old room dog in the army. to do things in a different way is not wrong as long as I am not preventing others from doing what they are doing or hurting someone in the process. I heard that concept from my father and also from one of my many mentors in life Simon Sinek.

Many may say or think that this is not a good choice to make but to be blunt I am not that concerned about what the masses think and I live my Life on my own terms! Before the printing press was invented we had to hand write everything in one form or another!! I told a high school classmate once that I write as if I am speaking directly to her. When we speak to a single person or in a group setting I have never seen or heard someone correct the speakers grammar or how they spelled a word.

this book is not going to be professionally edited either so effect this to be 100% authentic in content and in mistakes as well!! As my father often said in life "If you don't like the way I ~~took~~ look don't Look." With this Ideal in mind I pen this book not to please the masses but to share my story my way!!!

# Intro

In life most of us will have special people and mentors that have helped us learn and shaped us into the person we have become. I can not mention or dedicate this book to many but do dedicate this collection of my lifes memories to my family especially my veteran father and brothers who along with myself served our countries armed forces honorably for about 40 years as a family. I also pay special tribute to all former, present and future members of the armed services and their families that also secure freedom with the unspoken of sacrifices they make as well.

Last but not least as you will see in the content I share my memories about my time spent with Steve and our service days!

# My Childhood

I can remember as a small boy ages 6-12 my older brother and I had a least 100 or more play army men and vehicles. We would often set up a war zone to see who could win the latest battle. Countless hours were spent playing war games and we took those toys with us almost everywhere we went. I still remember setting up at my aunt's house on her staircase.

My father who was in basic training at the end of WWII did not often speak about it but had a few stories about his service days. He did have a few items he brought back from the war and would on occasion show us. He had a WWI bayonet he hung on a wall after mom died and he got into his own place around age 82.

I was born pigeon-toed and had some leg and feet problems and would easily trip when walking when I was real young. My feet were not straight and turned into each other. The doctors at the time had special footwear created for me to force over a long period of time my body to straighten my bones to a more normal position.

As a child I had countless sleepless/restless nights because of the mild pain it took to force my bones to straighten out.

# My childhood

My doctors forced me to avoid all contact sports that could hurt my legs. this was a issue and hard on me to see my brother and friends playing football and all I could do was watch.

Finally at the age of 15 my leg doctor decided that the danger to my legs was over and though I was not 100% corrected I could stop using the special footwear and play football or any other contact sports. that was the best news in my life up to that point and I have been a driven person from that time on!! I did play baseball and did OK but signed up for football the first chance I got even though I had no clue or experience in that sport.

the coach new I had no past experience but let me join the team and it was a life changer for me. If I had been in a larger school district the chances are high I would not have been able to participate! I was one of the shortest and smallest guys on the team at 5'6" and 135 lbs! After being forced all those years to just watch I was determined to not let anyone out sprint me. for the most part I was always at the front of the pack during sprints. I considered that to be acceptable because being shorter my gate did not cover as much ground as others but I was beating most guys anyway!!

5

# My childhood

I have not told anyone about my leg issues, except one high school friend 30 plus years after graduation. Because I did not want to be treated any differently than anyone else in life!

Most young boy's want to become a ninja or martial arts master so they could kick the bad guys butts. I was no exception to this so my neighbor and I would get the martial arts magazines and study the moves and he made drawings of them for me. I still have a few of them to this day.

Being in a small town in the 1980's there were very few if any martial arts schools around that I could attend. After I got the ok from my doctor to participate in contact activities I did search for any martial arts schools in my area. Finally I found a article in a newpaper for a karate school that was holding classes in my area. So I showed my parents and kinda bugged them to let me join the class.

Prior to finding this class my cousin who was a Airforce veteran showed me some basic moves he leared in the service and introduced me to my favorite martial arts weapon the nunchaku or numchucks as it is usually pronounced. I asked a different cousin of mine to try a karate class with me.

# My childhood

We found out that the workouts were hard and he soon quit but I stayed determined to become a black belt some day! After a bit I actually enjoyed the crazy workouts but they were even more difficult during football season and the workouts after school then two hours later I was in class 3 nights a week.

As a typical 16 year old I would go to a party or two and drank a beer or two but passed on the pot. I remember well the night my cousin and I stole a fifth of Jack Daniels from his fathers liquor cabinet and slared it walking down the railroad tracks. Not long after we finished it I was sick as a dog not doing so good!!! the worst drunk in my life to date and that changed my mind on trying to get on purpose that drunk.

After I joined karate I stopped going out on friday nights with friends and spent my time in the dojo (training hall) for 2hrs. Class was 3 nights a week year round and I was extremly dedicated on going to class. After a bit a older guy from class would pick me up until I got my drivers licence!

My desire to be a soldier never left me despite my leg and feet issues not being fully corrected. So I took the military written test and passed it.

7

# my childhood

After I passed the test I was a happy camper that my chance to be a soldier was not crushed by outside of my control circumstances.
At this time the army offered a program called ~~delayed entry~~ delayed entry in witch you sign up 1 year prior to graduation from high school. I also had to pass the military physical and I somehow did!! All I had to do was pass high school and I would be Army bound.

AFter graduation I trained really hard so I would be in shape for infantry boot camp. the other passion I had as a youth was music and I was a drummer. Later in life when my first born son was in elementary band he volunteered me to help. the band teacher asked me to help with and participate with the marching band and I did for several years. I did help teach the kids the fundamentals of marching and the drum cadence we used for parades.

the elemetary dand teacher was also the drama club music director and she asked me to play my drum set for the pit band used in the drama clubs musicals. I had a blast working with the drama club for years as their drummer. One of my fond memories of high school was in my Senior Year at graduation time.

# My Childhood

At graduation it was a tradition to play one last time with the band. I had a drum set solo and a fellow band member wrote in my yearbook (in jest) that my solo sucked!! Being who I am I stayed after school almost every day for an hour and a half till I had the whole movement about fully memorized and not just my solo. It's a good thing I did because my ~~because my~~ percussion band mates forgot my sheet music the day of graduation and I had to play by memory only in front of an audience of ~~two~~ 3 hundred or so.

We all have a teacher that we like the best and I would say it was my gym teacher and coach. Looking back at high school and my teen years I have come to the conclusion that we all were just trying our best to fit in and understand what life was about.

At graduation I recieved the award for best attendance and I have my report cards to share with you a record I believe that may have never been beaten since! I am only missing one report card from grades 6-12 and in those years I only missed 2 days of school. I also found a 3rd grade report card and that was a ~~zero~~ few missed days as well. I was next to the youngest of 4 in the house and I got everyone else up for school!!!

9

my attendance records minus 8th grade report card!

Grade 6

Borg J.    Bobby    Paul A.

## Hoosick Falls Central School
### GRADES 4 - 5 - 6

A Message to Parents:

The instructional program of the HFCS is planned to provide the best possible education for each child in our district. A carefully planned course of study serves as a guide for promoting continuous growth in the basic skills. The school is also concerned with the mental, physical, emotional, and social growth of each child. You are invited to discuss your child's progress with his teacher or the principal whenever the need arises. By working together, the home and the school can keep a constant check on the child's development and progress in all areas.

Name .....................................

Teacher .....................................

Year ......1978 - 1979.....

George D

| EMOTIONAL AND SOCIAL ADJUSTMENT | 1 | 2 | 3 | 4 | 5 | 6 |
|---|---|---|---|---|---|---|
| 1. Gets along with others | S | S | S | S | S | S |
| 2. Obeys promptly and cheerfully | S | S | S | S | S | S |
| 3. Is courteous in speech and action | S | S | S | S | S | S |
| 4. Cooperates in classroom activities | S | S | S | S | S | S |
| 5. Is attentive in classroom | S | S | S | S | S | S |

| WORK HABITS AND ATTITUDES | | | | | | |
|---|---|---|---|---|---|---|
| 1. Begins and completes work promptly | S | S | S | S | S | S |
| 2. Produces neat and careful work | S | N | S | S | S | S |
| 3. Uses time and materials wisely | N | S | S | S | S | S |
| 4. Works well in group activities | S | S | S | S | S | S |
| 5. Listens to, and follows directions | S | S | S | S | S | S |
| 6. Depends on himself when possible | S | S | S | S | S | S |
| 7. Tries to improve constantly | N | S | S | N | N | S |
| 8. Works to capacity | N | S | N | N | N | S |
| 9. Participates in class discussion | S | S | S | S | S | S |
| 10. Takes pride in his work | N | S | S | S | S | S |

| ATTENDANCE RECORD | | | | | | |
|---|---|---|---|---|---|---|
| Days Present | 28 | 29 | 39 | 29 | 27 | 33 |
| Days Absent | 0 | 2 | 0 | 0 | 0 | 0 |

# HOOSICK FALLS·CENTRAL SCHOOL

## REPORT OF PROGRESS

Grades 7 - 8

19....19.. 19.87......

HASKELL, ALAN
Student's Name

Miss Eddy                                    112
Homeroom Teacher                             Room

PROMOTED

To Parents:

This report is sent to you every six weeks to keep you informed of your child's progress in school. Academic marks are a combination of tests, classwork and homework. A minimum passing is often given to pupils who are working to the best of their ability. Parents should realize that this minimum mark is not acceptable to colleges or to many business establishments.

If there are questions concerning grades given, an individual conference with the teacher should be arranged. A convenient conference time can be set by calling the principal or guidance counselor. The principal, teachers and guidance counselor welcome the opportunity to talk with you about your child's progress.

| | | | | | | | | | | | | | |
|---|---|---|---|---|---|---|---|---|---|---|---|---|---|
| Health | | / | | / | | / | | / | | / | | 90 | / |
| Physical Ed. | | | | | | | | | | | | | |
| Days Absent | 0 | | 0 | | 0 | | 0 | | 0 | | | | Total |
| Days Tardy | | | | | | | | | | | | | |

11

# HOOSICK FALLS CENTRAL SCHOOL

## REPORT OF PROGRESS

Grade 9

19.....81.   19.....82..

HASKELL, ALAN
Student's Name

Mr. Betts _____ 206
Homeroom Teacher                Room

To Parents:

This report is sent to you every six weeks to keep you informed of your child's progress in school. Academic marks are a combination of tests, classwork and homework. A minimum passing is often given to pupils who are working to the best of their ability. Parents should realize that this minimum mark is not acceptable to colleges or to many business establishments.

If there are questions concerning grades given, an individual conference with the teacher should be arranged. A convenient conference time can be set by calling the principal or guidance counselor. The principal, teachers and guidance counselor welcome the opportunity to talk with you about your child's progress.

| | | | | | | | | | | | | | | |
|---|---|---|---|---|---|---|---|---|---|---|---|---|---|---|
| Band | | | | | | | | | | | | | | / |
| Physical Ed. | | | | | | | | | | | | | | ¼ |
| Days Absent | 0 | | 0 | | 0 | | | | | | | | | Total |
| Days Tardy | | | | | | | | | | | | | | |

12

# HOOSICK FALLS CENTRAL SCHOOL

## REPORT OF PROGRESS

Grade 10

19...82.. 19...83...

HASKELL, ALAN
_____
Student's Name


Mr. Betts                          206
_____
Homeroom Teacher                   Room


Guidance Counselor:   Mr. Brewster ✓
                      Miss Roman


To Parents:

This report is sent to you every six weeks to keep you informed of your child's progress in school. Academic marks are a combination of tests, classwork and homework. A minimum passing is often given to pupils who are working to the best of their ability. Parents should realize that this minimum mark is not acceptable to colleges or to many business establishments.

If there are questions concerning grades given, an individual conference with the teacher should be arranged. A convenient conference time can be set by calling the principal or guidance counselor. The principal, teachers and guidance counselor welcome the opportunity to talk with you about your child's progress.

| | | | | | | | | | | | | | | | | |
|---|---|---|---|---|---|---|---|---|---|---|---|---|---|---|---|---|
| Physical Ed. | | | | | | | | | | | | | | | | ¼ |
| Days Absent | _ | | ~ | | ~ | | ✓ | | | | | | | | | Total |
| Days Tardy | ~ | | \ | | | | ~ | | | | | | | | | |

13

# HOOSICK FALLS CENTRAL SCHOOL

## REPORT OF PROGRESS

Grade 11

19...83... 19..84...

ALAN HASKELL
_____
Student's Name

Mrs. Clintsman                    205
_____     _____
Homeroom Teacher              Room

Guidance Counselor:   Mr. Brewster
                      ~~Miss Roman~~

To Parents:

This report is sent to you every six weeks to keep you informed of your child's progress in school. Academic marks are a combination of tests, classwork and homework. A minimum passing is often given to pupils who are working to the best of their ability. Parents should realize that this minimum mark is not acceptable to colleges or to many business establishments.

If there are questions concerning grades given, an individual conference with the teacher should be arranged. A convenient conference time can be set by calling the principal or guidance counselor. The principal, teachers and guidance counselor welcome the opportunity to talk with you about your child's progress.

| Band | | | | | | | | | | | | $C_r$ | | 1 |
|------|---|---|---|---|---|---|---|---|---|---|---|---|---|---|
| Physical Ed. | | | | | | | | | | | | | | ¼ |
| Days Absent | O | O | O | | O | | O | | | | | | | Total |
| Days Tardy | | | | | | | | | | | | | | |

# HOOSICK FALLS CENTRAL SCHOOL

## REPORT OF PROGRESS

### Grade 12

### 19...84...  19..85....

---
HASKELL, ALAN
**Student's Name**

---
Mrs.Clintsman                                    205
Homeroom Teacher                              Room

Guidance Counselor:    Mr. Brewster
~~Miss Roman~~

To Parents:

This report is sent to you every six weeks to keep you informed of your child's progress in school. Academic marks are a combination of tests, classwork and homework. A minimum passing is often given to pupils who are working to the best of their ability. Parents should realize that this minimum mark is not acceptable to colleges or to many business establishments.

If there are questions concerning grades given, an individual conference with the teacher should be arranged. A convenient conference time can be set by calling the principal or guidance counselor. The principal, teachers and guidance counselor welcome the opportunity to talk with you about your child's progress.

| | | | | | | | | | | | | | | | |
|---|---|---|---|---|---|---|---|---|---|---|---|---|---|---|---|
| Band | | | | | | | | | | | | | | Cr. | 1 |
| Physical Ed. | | | | | | | | | | | | | | | ¼ |
| ys Absent | | | | | | | | | | | | | | | Total |
| ys Tardy | | | | | | | | | | | | | | | |

Age 18

Alan 1980

Shantung Black Tiger.

whirl wind kick.

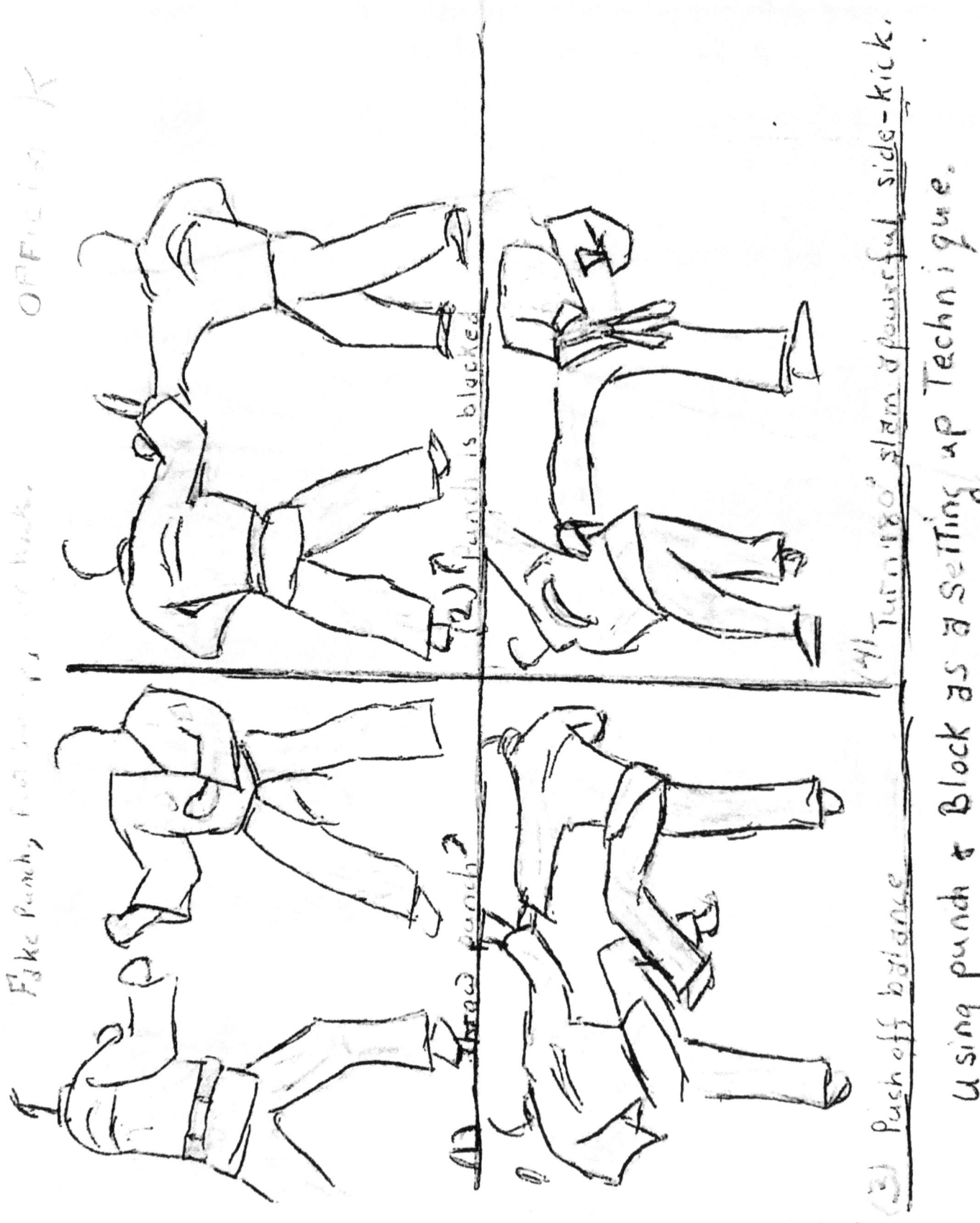

Fake Punch,            OFFICE K

(2) Fake punch is blocked

(3) throw punch

(4) Jujitso' slam & powerful side-kick.

(3) Push off balance

Using punch & Block as a Setting up Technique.

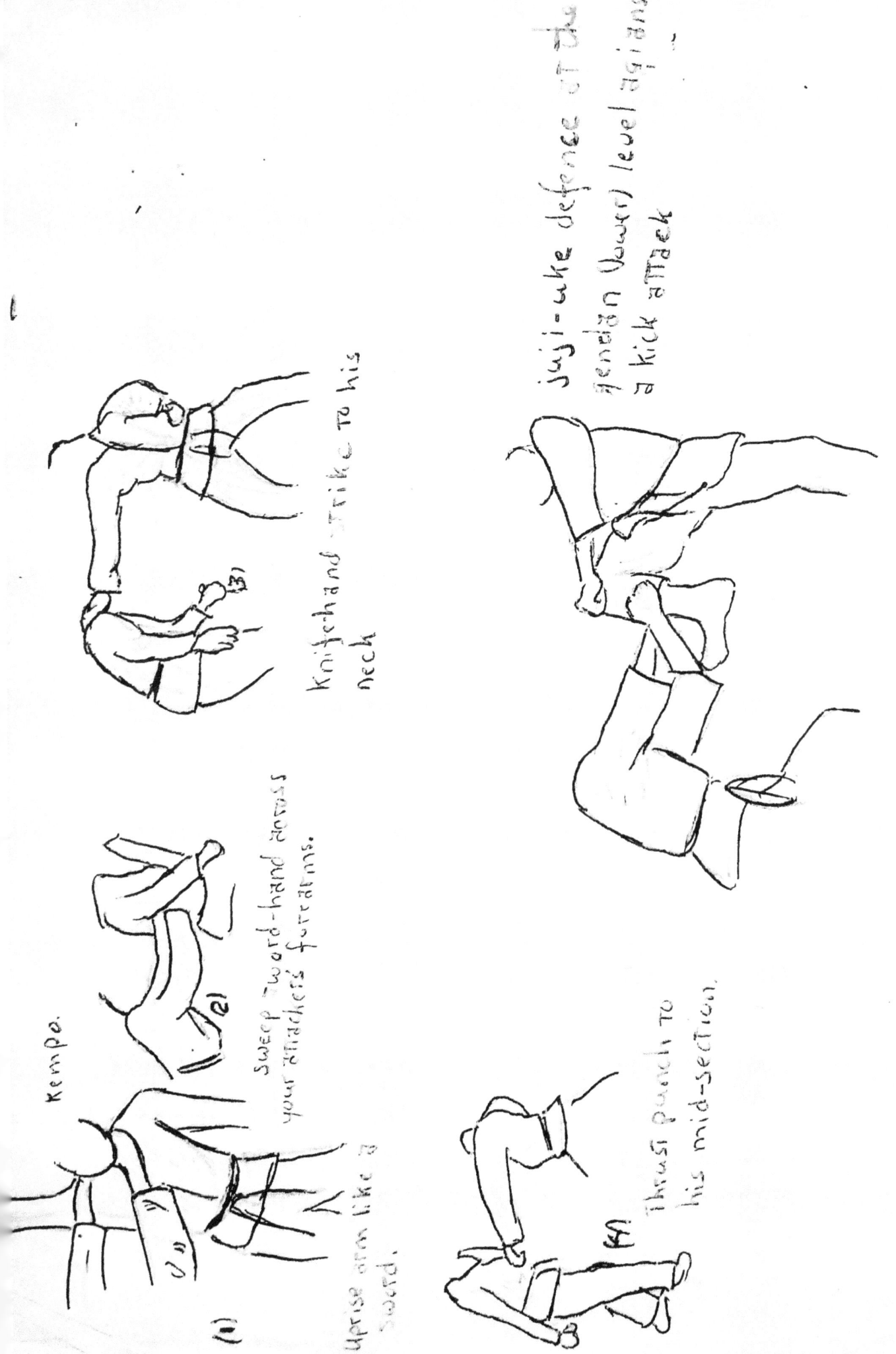

Kenpo.

(1) Uprise arm like a sword.

(2) Sweep-sword-hand across your attacker's forearms.

(3) Knife-hand strike to his neck.

(4) Thrust punch to his mid-section.

Juji-uke defence of the gendan (lower) level against a kick attack

19

## Basic training

Basic training started in August of 1985 in Fort Benning Georgia (home of the infantry). No matter how well you are prepared physically your mental and physical strength will be tested to the utmost limit.

The 20 months plus of traditional karate training helped a lot and I was not as mentally challenged as many of the other guys were but still to the limit!! I never faltered but many did and a few had to be sent home with a discharge stating the inability to adapt to military life.

The first day was processing and the famous buzz cut. After recieving all the necessary gear we were greeted by being herded like cattle onto a bus and sent to our new home for 3 month. When we arrived at the barracks a 6 foot plus D I (drill instructor) was pounding on the side of busses and was yelling get the F off the bus and line up. I kinda knew basic was not going to be a easy thing but that reality just hit home!

After a bus load of semi freaked out guys lined up we were told that we belonged to them now and your mama can't protect your candy asses no more. Sorry for the language but necessary for understanding!!

## Basis training

The next two statements were if you are a smoker too F-n bad you just quit and if you are a religious person this may not be the place for you but services will be provided in the near future.

We were then divided into small platoons and our DI's took us to our barracks to assign us bunks.

Our foot lockers stored our equiptment and day to day uniforms but our dress uniform had to be in a regular hang up closet to remain unwrinkled!

These barracks were still old style open bay rooms and bathroom. You would have to become verry comfortable doing your hygiene and bathroom needs with 40 other guys at the same time. I feel most guys viewed the first 2 months of basic as going through a living hell. It was a physical and mental torture that we had to endure as a team. All I can say is that you will be amazed at what we humans can survive as far as pain goes when we no longer focus on ourselves and put the needs of the team as a whole first.

Alone most us would never be able to handle the things infantry boot camp requires to become a soldier. Those soldiers who go into special ops endure the most to qualify for those teams!!

21

# Basic training

The mission of defending our country and our freedoms will alway take team work. Having the willingness to take the bullet in order to protect the nation and your fellow soldiers is what has kept America free!! Many have died in combat protecting freedom but we also have some that die in non combat situations and accidents as well. In our history we have had some extraordinary people do amazing things in battle but the mission in protecting our country will only be accomplished by being dedicated to the mission and eachother!

I can and still do recite to myself the phrase we were made to say prior to sitting down for every training class in boot camp.

"We Bust Our ASS to Make this class if Your Shit is Straight You Stay Awake if Your Shit is weak you Fall ASleeP. ECO 22 HeadHunters" I do recall this in my mind when things get tough in life and it reminds me that I have been through worse things than what the civilian life can be.

After basic training I was assigned to the
4th Battalion 41st Infantry (MECH) 2nd Armored
Division (FWD) in Germany. Being this was
my first ever trip overseas I was a bit nervous but
really excited at the same time. I was a newly
qualified soldier with only basic training education
but with a drive to be the best I could possibly be.
I diligently studied all the field manuals even
on the weekends when most everyone was out on
the town so that I was not unprepared in anything.
   I never missed a full day of duty my entire
two and a half years I was stationed in Germany
due to illness or pain from injuries that were
less than a broken leg etc. Suck it up is the
Infantry way and I still say to myself often
suck it up and deal soldier!! Bleeding feet, broken
blisters, strains or sprains would never give me
a excuse to not do my duty because if in
combat you can't say time out enemy I am in
pain and let me rest a bit!!
   I only used sick call one time because I
was told to because I was barfing up during
a long run. they said I had a stomach bug so
I got some meds and was back on duty the
next morning.

23

Graduation date was 21 November 1985

Conversation between two old room dogs

Steve seen my facebook post this year (2019)
and reached out to me. I was verry cautious about
who I friended or got messages from when I did use
social media.' I only knew it was him when he said
it was your old room dog because no other Person would
have known this unless they served with me in the
1980's. the time frame order of our conversations are
random but are 100% true in content minus a few
ettremely personal things not meant for public knowledge.
    In summary my facebook post stated that
all veterans to some degree come home with a form
of PtSD or other issues that in a way Prevent us
from returning mentally to the person we were
before we served. I also stated that the family
and friends who deal with our issues no matter
great or small are heroes to our country in their
own way especially those who have lost someone
to war. We also have Service members die in times of Peace!!!
    A very important conversation to me is as follows
Steve: When I went to the bulf war all my men came
back alive. It was hard and scary but I thought of you
over there and you got me through the war. I thorgh of
your actions in Germany and thank you best of all for
being my room dog. PS don't forget the saying when we
tried to hold you down.

25

# Conversation between two old room dogs

"I'm going to open a can of whoop ass on you".
Myself: Thanks for your bravery in the war and I wished I was over there with you and the rest of the forces. It means a lot to know that I got you through the war and I did make a difference in the way I was in the Company and our squad. I hope I did not give anyone the impression that I thought I was better than them and wanted to go to HQ to get away ~~from~~ from anybody. I have been a driven person my whole life and give 100% effort in everything I do not just being a soldier. Like you when I was in the guard I was teaching them things I knew well from being in the Army. My platoon SGt took me in his tank to be his gunner after a while and basically forced me to be the training NCO before I was promoted to SGt. Don't take this the wrong way but I am proud of you for the growth and leadership you showed in the Gulf war!!

Steve: I am proud of you for being there and when you went to HQ it was because you were a good soldier with skills. So people try to put you down when you do a good job so just be yourself and my veteran room dog.

Myself: truthfully for all these years I have had ~~an~~ occasional problems in my mind thinking that all my efforts and crazy (as I saw it) hardcore mindset was never appreciated by many of the

conversation between two old room dogs

Men that I served with. It does seem that many of the people in the civilian population care less about what it takes for us to be free and take their freedoms for granted!! You have released that burden from my mind knowing that I did have some positive impact on my fellow soldier and possibly contributing in some way saving the lives in the war defending freedom for others including our nation room dog.

I was really bummed for a while when I tried to re-enlist and go back to our old unit because I was told I could not. thanks for finding my face book post and reaching out. I was not sure it was you until you called me room dog. I have a civilian lady to thank for lending me a momentary ear and saying some encouraging words to me wherever she may be. Her kindness got me to open up with the face book post.

Steve: Well you inspired a lot of people in the Army. You gave me courage in the gulf war. when we did a flanking maneuver around the hill in Southern Germany and came upon the enemy and took them out when you were in charge of us that time. I did the same maneuver in the gulf war and came around an enemy hill that had 35 men with the 40 men I was in charge of and took them in one hour. Only one guy got wounded!

## Conversation between two old room dogs

It was your inspiration that gave me sucess in that military action

Family members don't realize what you and I and all veterans out there did to keep the country safe. You still inspire me today as you did back then so keep your drive and be creative in your book. Don't forget bulldog hill and those Monday runs. Have a great day for a great person. Later my room dog.

Myself: I have been giving a lot of thought about your comments about inspiration and I believe that your actions in the gulf war gave your men the courage to get the job done and come home as heroes like all who served in any wan you must give yourself credit for your own actions because true bravery comes from within. thanks for the comments it does make me feel good but don't downgrade yourself because you may have taken a piece of my warrior spirit with you but you developed your own and kicked ass with it bro!!! thats what true warriors and heroes do. I am honored to have been a part of the lives of all those I served with and to see my old room dog turn into the warrior knerrbo I knew he could be. Be proud of yourself and never let anyone's opinion of you get you down or change who you are to please them. Later bro

Conversation between two old room dogs

Steve: Remeber Graf and the mud pits.

Myself: A lifetime of mud at the wash racks when we returned from the field.

Steve: Remeber the laser equiptment on the Bradley's after the field cleaning botes of stuff fo hours with a toothbrush hated that. Remember you were repelling off the building in Southern Germany and your O ring came off and you fell around 15 feet.

Myself: Yup actually I have a slight tear in my left knees meniscus that was discovered in my 30's and my left hip has never been the same sense that fall. I was so mad at the Lt butterball new guy that hooked me up. It was not our Lt that messed up!! If you recall I was repelling Ausie style (back to the wall and more difficult to break). I think I was the only crazy enough guy to try Ausie style that day. It was a good thing that my belay man was out of the way and I did not drop directly on him. Drop and roll training came in real hard that day!

As I get older my left knee pains me on a regular basis. About a 2 or 3 on the pain scale most days but worse on the cement floors at work In my mind it is a small price to pay knowing I did my part to protect the freedoms of our nation family and those I personally know and care about.

29

Conversation between two old room dogs

Steve: Remember Graf we had to help dig out a Bradley that was stuck in the mud. It took 8 hrs and a big M88 tank recovery vehicle to get it out in 1987.

Myself: that wonderful mud hole. Not sure exactly when I was sent to HQ in 87 but do remember driving my M113 track for the XO. On that battalion trip a comrade died because his Bradley sunk in a huge mud hole filled with water. The driver never made it out and he drowned. I think it was a Company C guy!!! One of sad memories of those days!

Steve: we were in convoy with them and I was the 5th Bradley behind them and seen it plunge and sink down in the mud hole so I drove over to the tree line to the left and followed the trees and was safe but got in trouble for doing so.

Myself: If memory serves me the XO made me turn around and go back to make sure all the other Bradley's made it through and like you I took my track off the path to get to where I was told to go. It was not easy and the XO gave me complements on how I could handle my track in the trees without getting us stuck as well.

conversation between two old room dogs

If you remember anything else about our Army days don't be shy about it even if it's something negative about me. I am ok with negative feedback and need to know about it!! Have a good one room dog.

Steve: Remember Cross Swords and we had to go to the creek to wash off real Quick because no showers available. Froze my (Blank Blank) Off. Don't forget doing railhead duty shoveling the snow off the flat rail cars what a Job. Out there 6 hours before the train showed up and froze our ass off. I remember doing KP out in field in the pouring rain what misery. the one time we made 500 olive loaf sandwiches for everybody. I don't have any negative about you.

Myself: thanks for the info I remember most of that fun stuff and KP was great in the rain and in Denmark at 25 below zero doing dishes outside. the cold showers there as well.

Steve: Don't forget when we had to carry the tent poles and camo nets from the attic and unpack everything and count them and check the paPework just to Pack it all up again and carry it back upstairs. then the next week back at it again.

Myself: the real fun was setting nets in the field then cleaning them back of Post after we returned.

31

conversation between two old room dogs

Speaking of Cross Swords I exchanged a camo fatigue top with a Belgian soldier and still have it in the things I did not loose in the fire my parents had.

Steve: what was worse was the lasers from the Bradley's setting them up then taking them down and spending hours and days cleaning those things. what misery.

With a heavy heart I report that Steve passed away prior to the completion of this book. I will also say that the day his brother told me over the phone that he had died was the first time I ever in my life that I had a emotional reaction bad enough that I had to take time to compose myself before I could continue.

My future plan was to see him again after I had the book done and out for public view! His words to me to be creative in my book is a driving factor in hand printing this book because it's the most creative and daring thing I could do to honor our time spent together serving our country. RIP Knerrbo

the top I recieved from a soldier from Belgum
when "CROSS Swords" was over and we all got to
meet eachother and he recieved my BDU top as well!
BDU means battle dress uniform

the Lazer equiptment Strobe light on top of our Bradley that Steve mentioned. Steve is in backgrovnd of the two guys!

# Barracks Life during the Cold War

   The married soldiers lived off post so I
can't speak about that but do know that they
did have inspections on occasion.
   As a single soldier I was assigned to a
multi person room consisting of two or three guys.
When you first arrive straight out of basic training
you are basically fresh meat to the roommate
who has been there for a while. It is tradition to
mess with the newbies for a while to see what
they can handle and what they actuall understand.
   Being a private E-1 the higher ranking roommate
would be in charge of YOU and have a degree of
control over you but also be responsable for the
overall condition of the room. I did fall for a
trick or two but rather quickly held my ground.
   I did have about two years of karate training
in high school and I was not a pushover regardless
of anyone's size or rank under sergeant.
As in all situations in life when you stand
up to the bullies they typically back down. I
would practice in my room when I was alone
but was caught doing so and the so you think
your a bad ass tough guy attitude etisted for
a short time with a few of the guys. I do
not think or act as if I am better than others.   35

## barracks life during the cold war

I let my actions speak for me. When the new guy can keep up and in some cases out do my seasoned comrades in physical fitness they backed off quickly and I earned their respect as a fellow soldier. Fortunately I only had to prove myself once or twice publicly when I was challenged physically. I did warn guys like Steve said but there is always one or two that had to find out the hard way so to speak that I was not going to be anyone's punching bag! After that I was left alone and not messed with for the most part.

Having a squared away room at all times was a requirement not a suggestion!! Everything had to be within regulation or there would be some form of punishment/adjustments for everyone who occupied that room. This applied all week long but some slack was given on weekends we were off duty or in the field training. I got to know a buffer on a personal name bases with almost daily use while on post. Pop up inspections could happen at any time but when announced I was up all night till 2 or 3 am insuring my room was as perfect as possible. Many times I buffed the hallway as well.

Barracks Life during the Cold War

Seldom ever did any room in the entire company get a perfect inspection report. Later on when I was in charge of a room I would get my ass chewed a new one and a few extra pushups (HA HA) if I did not ensure my roommates stuff was up to regulation.

The regulations in my opinion were almost impossible to maintain on purpose. Complete and unquestionable discipline is what it takes to be amongst the best trained soldiers in the world with the exception to All special ops units like the Navy Seals, Army Rangers etc.

The day always started with a 5:30 Am formation and Pt when we were not in the field. On Monday's the CO would take us on what I and many others considered a death run to what he claimed as bulldog hill. This was the steepest and largest hill in the LTA (local training area) which was primarily used for combat training using the vehicles to get there. We were Bravo Company (bulldogs) in the battalion and once a month we had a battalion run and the battalion commander liked to also go out to bulldog hill and run the crap out of the whole battalion. When our company got to bulldog hill on battalion runs

37

# Barracks life durring the Cold war

our Company Commander made us break Formation and as a Company Sprint up the hill and get to the top of the hill before the battalion Commander got there. When I was moved to HQ I was tasked to carry the Company flag (guidon) on all runs and sprinting up hill was not a easy feat while carring the Company flag along with the required Flack Jacket (bullet proof vest).

After Pt was done we had to shower and get to the mess hall for some chow and be back in formation at 9 Am all spit shined and severed away to Start the day. I do recall as a teen hearing the Army slogan on tv stating that we do more before 9 Am than most people do all day.

Daily vehicle preparedness was vital so that was usually the first order of business of the day. All Bradley's were fully Combat loaded at all times to insure we were Capable of combat at a moment's notice. If anything were to go down a quick trip to the armory to get our personally assigned weapon and vehicle key's and take the fight to the enemy in a short period of time!

The post commander would on a regular bases call an alert in the early morning hours — 1 or 2 Am and the entire post needed to be ready to roll out within 2 hrs.

# Barracks Life durring the Cold War

Every unit on Post had to be ready for any form of sustained combat mission and have all the supplies needed to do so! Every man had a pre determined Job to make this happen. Let's not forget that we did not have cell phones or internet services and just had phones in the leaders offices and one at the CQ desk. Most all communication was accomplished by word of mouth until we got to the vehicles and the mounted radio in each track, Jeep or various vehicles used by the battalion.

Like all military Post their must be 24 hr 365 guard duty for the Post as a secured installation. Every battalion on Post had it's own motor pool that required the same level of guard duty. My battalion had billions of dollars worth of vehicles and equiptment to protect at all times. My battalion had 4 line companies tasked to guard the motor Pool so one week of the month when we were not in the field my company did guard duty!

typically 3 men were on duty at one time. One stayed in the guard shack at the one and only entry point on foot. One to check each ID as a soldier entered and one to walk the fence ~~fort~~ Perimeter continually!

Barracks Life durring the cold war

the guardshad a M16 on them and at times had live rounds if the threat level was high! the gate and walking guard would change place halfway throug the duty ~~shift~~ shift.

As I recall the sergeant of the guard and the guards would determine the length of the guard shift. Guard duty would be from 9 Am till 9 Am the next day. Because we always had more men than needed to pull guard duty we all had to be in formation to see who was the most squared away in uniform presentation and had to answer questions correctly in order to be dismissed from guard duty that day. the men who were dismissed just continued the normal tasked duty for the day and the others would report for guard duty.

We were not off the hook yet because the company had to do kP for the battalion mess hall at the same time as guard duty. No soldier under the rank of sergeant got out of kP and we all did our turn. No one escaped both guard duty and kP duty. kP was actually harder then guard duty most of the time.

MY WORD FAMOUS BUFFER. WE SPENT MANY A HOUR TOGETHER WHEN NOT IN FIELD TRAINING. STRIP THAN WAX AGAIN AND AGAIN AND AGAIN!!

# Squad duty

All squad members are assigned a specific weapon and task to ~~do~~ perform when we were on foot away from the vehicles. When I first got to Germany I was assigned to be a AG (assistant gunner) to the squads m60 machine gun gunner. My job was to learn and master the m60 beyond what was learned in basic training. At this time the assistant gunner was responsible for the tripod and to carry the extra amo neededfor the weapon, the tripod was needed for temporary fited positions to give the weapon the ability to easily swivel in any direction while being fired.

The AG's job was to be within feet of the gunner to assist or take over if the gunner was hit and unable to continue to pepper the enemy with lead!! the m60 was the main fire power of the squad on foot other than the Dragon anti tank weapon. Yes the guy with or around the machine gun would be the enemies first target to take out.

If you are afraid to die for your country or the men you are serving with my guess is that you should have never joined the Infantry to begin with!!!

42

## Squad Duty

I knew my PIG so well that I could take it apart and reassemble it blindfolded. The m60 weighs in at 23 lbs so when we hit the field with full combat gear on I was carrying almost half of my own body weight on maneuvers. Only in the movies do they make running with an m60 and the gear look easy. I can personally tell you it was the most physically challenging thing I have done and I was in top notch shape back then.

Along with the m60 I carried the m1911 .45 calaber handgun as my back up if the 60 was taken out or ran out of ammo and it came to hand to hand combat. If memory serves me I also had my bayonet. I lived for live fire day's with my 60 and 45!!! Just because I was the 60 gunner did not mean that I didn't have to remain proficient in every other weapon we used at that time. The law, clamor, the dragon, hand grenades etc were tested on a regular basis. My last qualifications in all the weapons were still better than needed to be a qualified infantry soldier."

Me and my M60 with blanks on a training mission in Germany. A mission auditor I think took this photo for me. The orange band was my teams color and the other Teams had other colors to identify them as well. The best 23-pound friend a soldier could have in a fire fight.

## Fellow Soldiers

Many fellow soldiers have had an important role in my youth and developement as a soldier but I will only give specifics about one. My platoon got a new Platoon Sergeant who became the NCO in charge of the platoon directly under the Lieutenant in charge. I knew something was different about him the first day he took over. He was as I recall the most able and fit leader I had up to that point. He was also the most laid back as far as uniform appearance goes but the CO and other officers seemed to not say anything to him publically anyway and let him be! As I recall in my mind he kinda took me under his wings so to speak in a mentoring roll rather quickly and dogged me out. He taught me a lot about my role as a machine gunner within his platoon and as a member of my squad as well

I made the biggest mistake of my young life when I told him that I did not think I could do something he wanted me to do because I was such a small guy. I am 5 foot 6 inches and in those days my weight was around 140 lbs! that day he not so politely adjusted my mindset on that that way of thinking. Mind over matter is a real thing in many things we believe that we can not do in life and this mindset is still active in my life to this day 36 plus years later!!!

# Fellow Soldiers

All humans have physical limitations fears or concerns and most of us stop when extreme pain hits us either physically or emotionally. Because of these pains and fears in life we often in our minds come up with many reasons why we must quit! the never give up or quit mentality has been with me most of my life and even more so after this fellow soldier came into my life. Sense about age 12 I have never backed down from guys in physical forms of challenge including football and my martial arts training and competitions. this is practically every guy in sports or in my years of karate competitions prior to and after I recieved my black belt level. In my system of karate I grew up in did not go by weight or size but by rank level for all forms of training or competitions.

When we had a general's inspection for the first time Sense this new platoon sergeant took over I finally got the picture so to speak of why he was more of a hard driving leader than some of the others in my platoon. He had on his dress uniform many ribbons and two unusually seen (At this time) awards in a mechanized infantry unit! He had a CIB (combat infantryman's badge) and a airborne pin!

# Fellow soldiers

I did ask him privately and he said that he was among those who did jump into Grenada and did some teaching within the Navy Seals but never again said a single word about it! After what I feel was a short time he left the platoon with no prior announcement in the same fashion as his arrival. When I was moved to HQ I recall asking top about him and he confirmed his basic info but said we could not talk about it and told me "enough said"!!! Everbody knows when top talks you don't just listen you obey! I have never spoken of this in over 30 year till Steve and I re connected in 2019. If you are interested in the historical event of the rescue of those college students simply look it up!

If I could see him, top the to and CO I would thank them all for all the things they taught me when I was in HQ for my last year serving in the Army. they all taught me things that the live soldiers were not privy to and I could not speak to about. they all helped me to become the best soldier I could be mind body and spirit! I still try to pass on this type of spirit to my fellow martial artist and students sense the day I returned home from the military.

# the USO and Lee Greenwood

I spent 30 months in Germany minus the month I spent at home with my parents for Christmas and my 21st birthday in 1987 and 1988 new years.

the U.S.O came to the base I was stationed at one time that I can recall. the Dallas Cowboy cheerleaders came and had lunch with us. that night these amazing Ladies put on a spectacular show for us. No words are needed to describe the atmosphere on Post that night.

I am taking a guess that I may be the only person from my home town that actually got to see a Live performance from the world famous Dallas Cowboy cheerleaders. I took many photos of them! this type of event does help troops feel that we are not for a few minutes taken for granted and some people back in the states do appreciate our sacrifice in keeping America safe and free!!

I remember as a kid seeing Bob Hope performing many times to support the troops. My dad never missed watching on television when Bob and other entertainers put on a televised show for the troops.

On Post we had a movie theater and we were made to go as a company to see a presentation of Lee Greenwoods song God Bless The USA. that song to this day gives me a feeling of gratitude that I still have the privilege to be living in America as a free Veteran. I can choose my own path in life because I live in a free Country!

At times I get very frustrated internally when I see people who abuse our nations programs to help those who are truly in need. of it. I have always believed in the old saying that you must work to get by in this life and nothing is for free. Yes I do understand some Just can't work! those who think that their Country owes them Just because they live here need to go for a time to a part of the world that does not even have the basics like clean water to drink!! Maybe then they will begin to appreciate what we have in America.

# Army Pay

I kept most of my paystubs and I will share four of them with the world. At this time all the money I recieved was mine because everything was provided for me.

We did have a recreation center on post and a gymnasium that were free so I saved a lot of money using them on most weekends we were not in the field! Unlike many of my fellow soldiers I did not go off post that often to the local town clubs and drink on the weekends. And that saved me a lot of money. I am guessing that the guys considered me to be a barracks rat and in a way that was probably true. I am glad I saved my money because that did allow me to go on two trips to etflore Amsterdam and Switzerland. I also saved to fly myself home for my 21st birthday and that alone took about 3 months of pay!!

Speaking of pay when I was chosen to be the XO's driver one of my HQ duties was to be payroll guard. From the bank to our barracks was about 1/8 of a mile. the XO had a brief case full of cash close to 100,000. dollars handcuffed to his wrist. Even on post I carried a loaded .45 pistol to guard him and the cash.

| 1. NAME (LAST, FIRST, MI) | | 2. UNIT ID CODE | TNG CAT CODE | 3. PAY GRADE | 4. PERIOD COVERED | |
|---|---|---|---|---|---|---|
| HASKELL ALAN D | | 4H225 | | E 1 | 01-31OCT85 | |

| 5. SOC. SEC. NO. | NET PAY DUE ⟹ | 558.00 | SUMMARY |
|---|---|---|---|

| | | | | | | 9. AMT BROT. FWD. | 51 |
|---|---|---|---|---|---|---|---|

| 6. ENTITLEMENTS | | 7. ALLOTMENT COLLECTIONS | | 8. OTHER COLLECTIONS | | 10. TOTAL ENT | |
|---|---|---|---|---|---|---|---|
| TYPE | AMOUNT | TYPE | AMOUNT | TYPE | AMOUNT | | |
| A BASIC PAY | 573 00 | | | SOLDIERHOM | 50 | 680 50 | |
| B REBATE | 6 90 | | | SGLI | 2 80 | 11. ALLOT COLLS | |
| C GIBIL | 100 00 | | | FEDERALTAX | 6 96 | | |
| D | | | | FICA TAX | 40 44 | 12. OTHER COLLS | |
| E | | | | STATE TAX | 18 06 | 122 76 | |
| F | | | | | | 13. NET EARN | |
| G | | | | | | 558 25 | |
| H | | | | | | 14. MID-MO PMT | |
| I | | | | | | NONE | |
| J | | | | | | 15. END MO PMT | |
| K | | | | | | 558 00 | |
| L | | | | | | 16. AMT TO BE BROT FWD | |
| TOTALS | 680 50 | | | | 122 76 | 25 | |

## TAX INFORMATION

| 17. ST & FED INC THIS PERIOD | 18. FED INC YEAR TO DATE | 19. FED TAX YEAR TO DATE | 20. FED EXEM | 21. FD ADD TAX WHD | 22. FICA WAGE | 23. FICA WAGE YEAR TO DATE | 24. FICA TAX YEAR TO DATE | 25. STATE CODE | 26. STATE EXEM | 27. ST ADD TAX WHD |
|---|---|---|---|---|---|---|---|---|---|---|
| 573 60 | 135752 | 15347 | S 0 | | 573 60 | 135752 | 9571 | NYT | S 0 | |

| STATE TAX | | LEAVE INFORMATION | | | | | ACCRUAL | | DEBT |
|---|---|---|---|---|---|---|---|---|---|

| 28. STATE INCOME YEAR TO DATE | 29. STATE TAX YEAR TO DATE | 30. BEG LV BAL | 31. LV EARN | 32. LV USED | 33. END LV BAL | 34. LV LOST | 35. LVPD | 36. MONTHLY ACCRUAL | 37. TOTAL ACCRUAL | 38. BALANCE DUE U.S. |
|---|---|---|---|---|---|---|---|---|---|---|
| 135752 | 4752 | 15 | 45 | | 60 | | | | | |

### 39

```
***AUG/85 IS FIRST RECORD MONTH ON COMPUTER
ITM6C O/COLL SEP 85 LES
CRA-ACCRUED THIS MO:     $.00 PD THIS MO:    $0.00 BAL:       $.00
```

REMARKS

## FINANCE OFFICE INFORMATION

| 40. DSSN | 41. CONTROL NUMBER | 42. SBDC | 43. OPED | 44. PEBD | 45. BASD/ASED | 46. TFOS | 47. YRS. | 48. ETS DATE | 49. PR NO. | 50. 7608 ADJ LV BALANCE |
|---|---|---|---|---|---|---|---|---|---|---|
| C089001882 | | MRN | 850820 | 8411 16 | 850820 | | 00 | 880319 | E2E | |

DA FORM 3686-1, AUG 83 For use of this form, see AR 37-104-3; the proponent agency is USAFAC.

◦ U.S. Government Printing Office: 1984-431-366

53

| 1. NAME (LAST, FIRST, MI) | 2. UNIT ID CODE | TNG CAT CODE | 3. PAY GRADE | 4. PERIOD COVERED |
|---|---|---|---|---|
| HASKELL ALAN B | AR7B0A | | E 2 | 01-28FEB86 |

| 5. SOC. SEC. NO. | NET PAY DUE ⟶ | 524.00 | 9. AMT BROT. FWD. |
|---|---|---|---|
| | | | 94 |

| 6. ENTITLEMENTS | | 7. ALLOTMENT COLLECTIONS | | 8. OTHER COLLECTIONS | | |
|---|---|---|---|---|---|---|
| TYPE | AMOUNT | TYPE | AMOUNT | TYPE | AMOUNT | |
| A BASIC PAY | 66738 | CFC  01 | 200 | SOLDIERHOM. | 50 | **10. TOTAL ENT** 67439 |
| B REBATE | 701 | | | SGLI | 400 | **11. ALLOT COLLS** 200 |
| C | | | | FEDERAL TAX | 7410 | **12. OTHER COLLS** 14928 |
| D | | | | FICA TAX | 4772 | |
| E | | | | STATE TAX | 2296 | **13. NET EARN** 52405 |
| F | | | | | | |
| G | | | | | | **14. MID-MO PMT** NONE |
| H | | | | | | |
| I | | | | | | **15. END MO PMT** 52400 |
| J | | | | | | |
| K | | | | | | **16. AMT TO BE BROT FWD** 05 |
| L | | | | | | |
| TOTALS | 67439 | | 200 | | 14928 | |

## TAX INFORMATION

| 17. ST & FED INC THIS PERIOD | 18. FED INC YEAR TO DATE | 19. FED TAX YEAR TO DATE | 20. FED EXEM | 21. FD. ADD TAX WHD | 22. FICA WAGE | 23. FICA WAGE YEAR TO DATE | 24. FICA TAX YEAR TO DATE | 25. STATE CODE | 26. STATE EXEM | 27. ST ADD TAX WHD |
|---|---|---|---|---|---|---|---|---|---|---|
| 66738 | 130638 | 14394 | S 0 | | 66738 | 130638 | 9341 | NYT | S 0 | |

| STATE TAX | | LEAVE INFORMATION | | | | | ACCRUAL | | DEBT |
|---|---|---|---|---|---|---|---|---|---|

| 28. STATE INCOME YEAR TO DATE | 29. STATE TAX YEAR TO DATE | 30. BEG LV BAL | 31. LV EARN | 32. LV USED | 33. END LV BAL | 34. LV LOST | 35. LVPD | 36. MONTHLY ACCRUAL | 37. TOTAL ACCRUAL | 38. BALANCE DUE U.S. |
|---|---|---|---|---|---|---|---|---|---|---|
| 130638 | 4429 | 35 | 125 | 13 | 30 | | | | | |

39

```
      EOM PAY OPTION - CHECK TO UNIT  AR7B0A
86-220 PROM        E02
86-219 COMP 6 MOS  OTHER-PAY
SAWLS GE168 EDEP COLA              GERMANY LOWER SAXONY
CRA-ACCRUED THIS MO:    $3.52 PD THIS MO:    $0.00 BAL:        $3.52
```

R E M A R K S

## FINANCE OFFICE INFORMATION

| 40. DSSN | 41. CONTROL NUMBER | 42. SSDC | 43. OPED | 44. PEBD | 45. BASD/ASED | 46. TFOS | 47. YRS. | 48. ETS DATE | 49. PR. NO | 50. 7800 ADJ LV BALANCE |
|---|---|---|---|---|---|---|---|---|---|---|
| 6393 | 001462 | MPN | 850820 | 841116 | 850820 | | 01 | 800819 | ELB | |

DA FORM 3686-1, AUG 83 For use of this form, see AR 37-104-3; the proponent agency is USAFAC.

«U.S. Government Printing Office: 1984-431-366

**MEMBER**

| 1. NAME (LAST, FIRST, MI) | | 2. UNIT ID CODE | TNG CAT CODE | 3. PAY GRADE | 4. PERIOD COVERED |
|---|---|---|---|---|---|
| HASKELL ALAN B | | AR7BOA | | E 3 | 01-31AUG86 |

| 5. SOC. SEC. NO. | NET PAY DUE ➡ | 663.00 | 9. AMT BROT. FWD. SUMMARY 99 |
|---|---|---|---|

| 6. ENTITLEMENTS | | 7. ALLOTMENT COLLECTIONS | | 8. OTHER COLLECTIONS | | |
|---|---|---|---|---|---|---|
| TYPE | AMOUNT | TYPE | AMOUNT | TYPE | AMOUNT | |
| A BASIC PAY | 74460 | AER-C 01 | 300 | SOLDIERHOM | 50 | 10. TOTAL ENT 84283 |
| B BASIC PAY | 1504 | CFC 01 | 200 | SGLI | 400 | 11. ALLOT COLLS |
| C REBATE | 32 | | | FEDERALTAX | 8794 | 500 |
| D REBATE | 780 | | | FICA TAX | 5432 | 12. OTHER COLLS |
| E COLA | 1395 | | | STATE TAX | 2825 | 17501 |
| F CLOTHNGALW | 6112 | | | | | 13. NET EARN |
| G | | | | | | 66381 |
| H | | | | | | 14. MID-MO PMT |
| I | | | | | | NONE |
| J | | | | | | 15. END MO PMT |
| K | | | | | | 66300 |
| L | | | | | | 16. AMT TO BE BROT FWD |
| TOTALS | 84283 | | 500 | | 17501 | 81 |

TAX INFORMATION

| | 17. ST & FED INC THIS PERIOD | 18. FED INC YEAR TO DATE | 19. FED TAX YEAR TO DATE | 20. FED EXEM | 21. FD ADD TAX WHD | 22. FICA WAGE | 23 FICA WAGE YEAR TO DATE | 24 FICA TAX YEAR TO DATE | 25 STATE CODE | 26. STATE EXEM | 27 ST ADD TAX WHD |
|---|---|---|---|---|---|---|---|---|---|---|---|
| TAX | 75964 | 551102 | 61858 | S 0 | | 75964 | 551102 | 39464 | NY | S 0 |

| STATE TAX | | LEAVE INFORMATION | | | | | ACCRUAL | | DEBT |
|---|---|---|---|---|---|---|---|---|---|
| | 28. STATE INCOME YEAR TO DATE | 29. STATE TAX YEAR TO DATE | 30. BEG LV BAL | 31 LV EARN | 32. LV USED | 33. END LV BAL | 34 LV LOST | 35 LVPD | 36. MONTHLY ACCRUAL | 37. TOTAL ACCRUAL | 38 BALANCE DUE US |
| MISC | 551102 | 19449 | 35 | 275 | 13 | 180 | | | | | |

39

```
     REMEMBER SEA POW/MIA'S ON 19 SEP, THEIR NATL RECOGNITION DAY
          EOM PAY OPTION - CHECK TO UNIT  AR7BOA
     ITM6B  DIFF PAY FOR  BASIC PAY        JUL 86
     ITM6C  DIFF PAY FOR  REBATE           JUL 86
R  860715 PROM       E03           8018856393
E  SAWLS GE168 CDEP COLA           GERMANY LOWER SAXONY
M  CRA-ACCRUED THIS MO:   $9.60 PD THIS MO:  $61.12 BAL:          $.00
A
R
K
S
```

FINANCE OFFICE INFORMATION

| | 40. DSSN | 41. CONTROL NUMBER | 42. SSDC | 43. OPED | 44. PEBD | 45. BASD/ASED | 46. TFOS | 47.YRS. | 48. ETS DATE | 49. PR NO | 50 7608 ADJ LV BALANCE |
|---|---|---|---|---|---|---|---|---|---|---|---|
| SVC | 6393 | 002121 | MPN | 850820 | 841116 | 850820 | | 01 | 880819 | ELB | |

DA FORM 3686-1, AUG 83 For use of this form, see AR 37-104-3; the proponent agency is USAFAC.

55

| 1. NAME (LAST, FIRST, MI) | | 2. UNIT ID CODE | ING CAT CODE | 3. PAY GRADE | 4. PERIOD COVERED |
|---|---|---|---|---|---|
| HASKELL ALAN S | | AR7BDA | | E 4 | 01-31JAN87 |

| 5. SOC. SEC. NO. | NET PAY DUE ➡ | 691.00 | SUMMARY |
|---|---|---|---|
| | | | 9. AMT BROT. FWD. 01 |

| 6. ENTITLEMENTS | | 7. ALLOTMENT COLLECTIONS | | 8. OTHER COLLECTIONS | | |
|---|---|---|---|---|---|---|
| TYPE | AMOUNT | TYPE | AMOUNT | TYPE | AMOUNT | 10. TOTAL ENT |
| A BASIC PAY | 65950 | AER-C 01 | 300 | SOLDIERHOM | 50 | 92265 |
| B BASIC PAY | 3630 | CFC 02 | 400 | SGLI | 400 | 11. ALLOT COLLS 700 |
| C REBATE | 22 | | | FEDERALTAX | 12042 | |
| D REBATE | 810 | | | FICA TAX | 6405 | 12. OTHER COLLS |
| E COLA | 1353 | | | STATE TAX | 3559 | 22456 |
| F | | | | | | 13. NET EARN |
| G | | | | | | 69110 |
| H | | | | | | 14. MID-MO PMT |
| I | | | | | | NONE |
| J | | | | | | 15. END MO PMT |
| K | | | | | | 69100 |
| L | | | | | | 16. AMT TO BE BROT FWD |
| TOTALS | 92265 | | 700 | | 22456 | 10 |

TAX INFORMATION

| | 17. ST & FED INC THIS PERIOD | 18. FED INC YEAR TO DATE | 19. FED TAX YEAR TO DATE | 20. FED EXEM | 21. FD ADD TAX WHD | 22. FICA WAGE | 23. FICA WAGE YEAR TO DATE | 24. FICA TAX YEAR TO DATE | 25. STATE CODE | 26. STATE EXEM | 27. ST ADD TAX WHD |
|---|---|---|---|---|---|---|---|---|---|---|---|
| TAX | 89580 | 89580 | 12042 | 0 | | 89580 | 89580 | 6405 | NYT | S | 0 |

| STATE TAX | | LEAVE INFORMATION | | | | | ACCRUAL | | DEBT |
|---|---|---|---|---|---|---|---|---|---|

| | 28. STATE INCOME YEAR TO DATE | 29. STATE TAX YEAR TO DATE | 30. BEG LV BAL | 31. LV EARN | 32. LV USED | 33. END LV BAL | 34. LV LOST | 35. LVPD | 36. MONTHLY ACCRUAL | 37. TOTAL ACCRUAL | 38. BALANCE DUE US |
|---|---|---|---|---|---|---|---|---|---|---|---|
| MISC | 89580 | 3559 | 205 | 100 | | 305 | | | | | |

```
39
         SEE YOUR UNIT TAX ADVISOR FOR FREE TAX PREPARATION.
         EOM        HOME & CITY SAV BK         CR 0630000015231
                    ALBANY NY              12207 DIRECT DEPOSIT
    ITM6B  DIFF PAY FOR  BASIC PAY        DEC 86
    1TM6C  DIFF PAY FOR  REBATE           DEC 86
    861209 PROM          E04
    861231 STOP COLA                      1111110015
    870101 AUTH COLA        GE403 9       1111110015
    870116 CHG  COLA        GE403 9         RATE CHG
    ALOT  CFC  02    4.00 BEG JAN87 WILL STOP  DEC87 BY 6393
    SAWLS GE403 DDEP COLA           GERMANY GARLSTEDT [LS]
    CPA-ACCRUED THIS MO: $10.20 PD THIS MO:  $0.00 BAL:    $50.40
```

FINANCE OFFICE INFORMATION

| | 40. DSSN | 41. CONTROL NUMBER | 42. SSDC | 43. OPED | 44. PEBD | 45. BASDVASED | 46. TFOS | 47. YRS | 48. ETS DATE | 49. PR NO. | 50. 7509 ADJ LV BALANCE |
|---|---|---|---|---|---|---|---|---|---|---|---|
| SVC | 6393 | 002195 | MRN | 650820 | 841116 | 650820 | | | 02 | 880819 | ELB |

DA FORM 3666-1, AUG 83 For use of this form, see AR 37-104-3; the proponent agency is USAFAC

# traveling by train

I believe that my Post Luscious D Clay kaserne was one of the most northern army post in Germany in the mid 1980's. We had to travel South for many of our training Locations so we had to travel by train.

The German rail system always placed us on the Lowest priority list for train movements. Because it took so Long we usually recieved sleeper cars to travel. The flatbed rail cars were just wide enough to drive the Bradley's on to them so there was very Little room for error.

As always there was guard duty on the train especially while stopped. I did my fair share of guard duty while traveling by train and when the threat level was high enough we would have live ammo ready to go if needed. I was amongst the few that were trusted with having live ammo on guard duty while traveling by train.

German citizens especially the kids would be gathered around and looking at the vehicles and troops that dismounted the train while we were stopped. We were given strict orders not to interact with anyone but some guys would toss out of the windows MRE'S to the kids when we started moving again! the CO did not say much because it was not physical interaction and in a way a tradition to do so!

A LIGHT MOMENT ON A TRAIN TRIP FOR TRANING IN SOUTHERN GERMANY. THE BEST LOOKING GLASSES I EVER OWNED (HA,HA,).

the Flatbed rail cars used when we traveled by train.
the Bradley took up about 90% of the width of
the rail car!

# Extreme Cold Weather training

Once a year we would take a trip to Denmark at a certain training location for two weeks to conduct extreme cold weather training. talk about cold the barracks we stayed in got to about 45° as a high temperature. the outside temerature was for the most part around 25° below zero on a warm day but did go Lower as well!

The problem at that Low of a temperature was in keeping the weapons warm enough to be able to fire and was the most challenging live fire ever! We had to be Prepared to face any enemy in a etreme cold enviroment. So Living in upstate New York with its winter weather is not that bad to me anymore after several field trips in Denmark!

The one time that having to Lug around the cold weather gear and equiptment was worth the xtra effort was in Denmark. the gear was a bit bulky at that time but it Literally saved our lives in Such Low temperatures. I did mention in my Conversation with Steve that I did dishes outside in Denmark. that I will guess is an experience that verry few People will ever have. the rubber gloves I had to do dishes did not do a good job keeping my hands warm but because of the

## Extreme cold weather training

hot wash ~~water~~ water my hands did not get
frostbitten but wer very cold to say the least.

At this time we used 55 gallon steel drums
for the wash and rinse water for doing dishes
in the field. the water was heated with old style
submersion heaters. these heaters were simple but
but got the job done! Only a simplele fuel tank
with a constant drip and a venting pipe for the
etavst was all that was used. Easy to set up and
easy to move is a must for a mobile mess hall in
a field environment.

Most all places that I was in I would have
a old 1980's disposable style camera to take pictures
with for my memories but I did not think it would
be able to handle the subzero temperatures so I
did not have one with me in those Denmark
training locations. All the photos in this book
were tooken with a disposable camera from the
1980's. the vast majority of my photos were taken
prior to my year in HQ working for the XO.

My duties in HQ were more sensitive let's say
so no photos taken for most things I was doing
and responsible for!!!

# NBC training

NBC is the term that was used for our
Nuclear Biological and Chemical training.
I am fairly sure most have heard of or about how
the military personal used gas chambers to train us
how to use our gas masks! My guess is that it was
not the favorite part of anyones training. this
was not a one and done training either.

As far as the gas chamber was concerned it was
big enough for about 30 people at a time. We would
go in with our masks on to be sure we had a good
protective seal and could not smell and of the gas.

After a few minutes we all had to remove our
mask so we would be exposed to the gas long enough
to start feeling the affects of it then put our
masks back on to insure we could do that under
pressure of the gas causing issues for us! the
guys who could not do that well enough to clear the
gas from their face quick enough would soon be
running for the exit and soon lost the contents
of their last meal (HA HA). Don't forget the
burning eyes and the exploding nose fun as well !!!

In this modern times people are hooked up to
a machine that tells us if ones mask is not
sealing well. But the kicker was that after all of
us got to take off our mask anyway and speak
out loud your name and rank before we could leave !!

# NBC training

the gas mask was part of our standard gear.
Also at random times while we were on company
road marches on foot we would be attacked with
CS gas canisters and others running all around us
with CS gas canisters attached to polls so all of
us got a dose of gas at the same time.

the first sign of the attack anyone could
yell and are trained to yell GAS GAS GAS
loud and fast so the whole company hear the call.
At the sound of this call everyone stoped moving
stopped breathing and closed your eyes untill you
had your masks on and ready for battle!

this was the C portion of NBC.

the nuclear part was not as cut and dry!
It was only simulated for obvious reason.
If you see ore hear a blast you needed to hit
the ground facing it and prepare for the
energy and destructive wave of air and debris.
If you did survive that you needed to turn around
and face the opposite direction for the possible
return of a wave!

We also used MOPP Gear a lot during field
training. I showed a picture of guys in their mopp
suit in the Bradley side view part of this
book. the MOPP suit is outer protective wear against
chemical attacks.

# NBC training

I do recall going hours totaly buttoned up inside a Bradley in full moPP gear from head to toe as if we were in a full blown chemical attack. We had a station set up for velicle and man chemical decontamination. this was no easy task doing combat training in full moPP Gear!

Feeling like the Company Ginny Pig and go to

the time I spent in HQ was both an honor
and privilage but also had a few less than fun
moments. My memory is very clear on the day I
had to be the live human the medics got to
practice on to learn how to perform a live IV
in a simulated combat environment! the first SGt (top)
voluntold me to play the victim for the company
medics to poke me to insure they could do a live
IV line for medical evalvation. It was a pleasure (Ha-Ha)
to be a human pin cushion for the Company medics!

    We all know that having sterile water to drink
is vital to our health and in the army this is
especially important in a field environment. Everyone
I believe has seen water or other liquid tankers
before and realize that the one hatch to get into
one is not very large. Because I was one of the
smallest in size a 29 waist size you could never
guess who was voluntold to go inside a field
water buffalo to clean and sterrilize it. It take
about 180° to destroy the harmful bacteria and germs
for a clean tanker to be used for water.

    the first step was to do a complete spray down
of the inside of the tanker with the hot water
one section of a time so the water would not
run on my bare feet. Once a section was cool

I would move to the next section. Next was to scrub it down with a special cleaner from top to bottom. The final rinse was a bit easier at the end because I was outside of the tanker to complete the task!

At this time we did not have bottled water so the old canteen was part of our standard equipment we carried. We did have 5 gallon steel containers that were on the vehicles for water supply in the field environment. So drinking is the priority over hygiene for the time spent in the field. Any small running brook was a welcome sight for hygiene needs!!! So when I hear people complaining about not having a shower for a day I say to myself at times thats nothing how about no running water at all for a week or two!!

Prior to being moved to HQ several of the guys in the company would ask me to iron their uniforms for inspections and shine boots as well. I made a few extra bucks on the side for that ability ( thanks mom. rest her soul). teaching a few grown men about laundry basics is a great lesson on the importance of making your children learn the fundamentals of life and not always doing things for them so they can take care of themselves as young adults! No parent is perfect and I am not but tried to instill the fundamentals life skills needed prior to my children graduating high school!

Company Ginny Pig and go to

Not sorry anyone but google can never ever replace hands on knowledge! Don't let google become your brain! Simply put no power or no interweb no brain!! Never be that person who can't funtion on your own brain power!

I was required to teach classes but at times a responsibility I did not want. When you are dealing with life and death knowledge the simplest mistake as a instructor could get someone killed when we used live explosives etc!! This is probably why I can be a real stickler for following safety rules at work and in life in general.

Serving Means, you lose your Personal freedom

From the day you first start boot camp till you
exit the Service the freedoms you enjoyed are put
on hold and you basically the property of the government
and you have little to no Personal choices in many
things. All who have served by choice go in the service
knowing this fact and knowingly put themselves in
harm's way to insure our nation is protected and
free.| I Personally chose the infantry with the
knowledge that it would be dangerous and I would
be on the frontline if war was to break out.
   By no means does this mean that front line soldiers
are more important than those who are not because it
takes every service member in all branches to
secure the freedoms of our nation! For one example
the Person who may be 3 thousand miles away from the
war zone controlling a drone by remote that drops
a bomb to take out a enemy target Is as vital as
those Personal in theater!
   My personal example of not having a Personal
choice is when the Powers to be decided to do
some budget cuts and my 18 month tour of duty
in Germany was extended to my ETS date. So
I did not have the opportunity to serve at
another base in my 3 year contract.

## Serving Means you lose your Personal Freedom

the only way to go back to the States was to take leave and Pay my own way home and I did Just that for my 21st birthday in 1988. For two years I never set foot on American soil due to a money saving cut in the military budget. I was real happy (Ha-Ha) with Congress that year!! there were several of us affected by this cut and were told only one month Prior to being assigned to a stateside duty station.

Also when I was moved to HQ within the Company and work for the XO and become the new company mail clerk it was on a voluntold basis. In my life I sometimes get a bit frustrated with people who complain about having to wait in Line at a store and have the nerve to get upset at the clerk who is Serving them.

When in the field we used what was called the Combat chow line. A hot meal in the field was a welcome thing!! To Perform a combat chow line only one person at a time was allowed to approach the mess station and get their food while all others in line were separated by about 10 feet, this separation is so that if we were to be attacked we would not be in groups and easily taken out.

Speaking of being in line I vividly recall one time the wife and I were checking out at a store and the older man in front of us was yelling at and belittling the teenage female clerk for making a mistake in the amount of change she gave him. She was only a few cents off and he acted as if she tried to cheat him on purpose.

As soon as he left she started to tear up and was as I see it feeling really bad about this situation. Immediately with a glance at the wife I knew it was ok for me to console this young lady with a hug that I knew she needed but asked her first and she was recieptive to the idea. I gave her a few words of encouragment without any worry about what other people would be thinking!!

After years of teaching and learning the martial arts along with plenty of self-education and reading books and articles about the human mind body and spirit I can take a fairly accurate guess at what a person is generally thinking and feeling by just body language alone. I could tell this young lady was in emotional pain and I had to help the best I could and she did respond with a smile before we left the checkout that day!

Serving means you lose your personal freedom

    I do believe that people can with training be able to heighten their abilities to sense in others the (generally speaking) emotions they are experiencing with just body language alone!

    The simple freedom to go shopping and purchase most anything we wish to is often taken for granted. Even in this time in history not all people have the freedom of choice that we have here in America and are still under some form of dictatorial persecution!

## the Russians and the Berlin Wall

Every year that I was stationed in Germany we would travel to Berlin to conduct M.O.U.n.t. (Military operations in urban terrain) training. I believe this site was called Doughboy City. We were so close to the border could almost throw a stone from that city training site over the fence to the Russian controlled side of East Berlin

I recall seeing a Hind-D (Russian attack helicopter) a time or two checking us out while we were training and they also had watch towers as wellb I can to this day recognize the Sound that a Hind-D makes with my eyes closed. this was the time in the Cold war area a few years before the Berlin Wall was torn down and the East side of Berlin was under the complete control of the Communist Russian government.

All ground forces had to train in urban warfare so we could be ready for battle in a city environment not just in wooded or open land environments. So we trained to be proficient in taking the fight to an enemy in buildings and also defending ourselves if we were occupying buildings. I believe if memory serves me that at this training location we also had to build teamwork because a large confidence course was there!

## the Russians and the Berlin wall

the only way we all could get through this course was by teamwork or we all failed and failure was not an option! Berlin will be a place that will never be forgotten in my memories because of the training and Check Point Charlie at the Berlin wall.

I believe it was in 1986 when we took a tour of East Berlin through Check Point Charlie. We were in dress uniforms and were permitted to watch the changing of the guard at the tomb of the Unknown Soldier close by in East Berlin. Also we toured the museum at the tomb of the unknown soldier that was guarded by Russian soldiers with their weapons shouldered.

My company traveled in a large army buss and we were watched by what I believed was the Russian KGB at that time in history. the only thing that was permitted for us to have on our bodies was East German Marks to spend in the shops and stores we were able to visit! the shops would not take the American dollar so we had to etchange our money in for East German marks prior to crossing through Check Point Charlie.

My habit of taking photos in most places I was in was haulted becouse we could not do that in East Berlin but I did take some

# the Russians and the Berlin wall

Pictures on the west side of the wall.

The one memory that has changed me forever happened just prior to departing on the buss back to West Berlin. For many years I had a bad dream on occasion about this. I was in line at a Ice cream vender and noticed a little girl and her mother a few people in line behind me. After I got my ice cream I had a handful of money I had not spent and did not wish to take it with me because it was only worth a few bucks in US currency. I was going to offer the little girl that money and tried to gesture that she could use it to buy her Ice cream. The mother of that little girl maybe 4-6 years old I was guessing looked at me as if I was trying to kill her and pulled her away from me. My guess is that it was highly frowned upon to be seen taking money from an American Soldier!! this was and still is very troubling for me to believe that a government can create such fear in their citizens that a simple gesture of kindness from a foreign soldier to a child in peace time would be considered a threat to them!

The Freedoms I have enjoyed my entire life up to that point took on a whole new meaning for me.

the Russians and the Berlin Wall

At times I believe this is the underlying reason I am compelled to teach ladies self-defense courses and in general try to be kind to women of all ages.

Sometimes I wish that every American citizen who has never completely lost all their freedoms for a bit of time could experience what it is to not have freedoms for a short period of time!

Maybe then people will understand how blessed we are to have them even though our governmetal system is far from perfect!! As a veteran my viewpoint may seem bias but I do fully believe that our freedoms only exist because of those who gave up their freedoms to protect and preserve it. the statement that All gave some and some gave all rings true for myself ever sense I returned home after my service days.

Speaking of this freedom to this day I will take the offertunity when I can to buy an Ice cream for any little girl I know the Parents of without fear or apprehension. I also many times buy Ice cream for all ladies within my family and secretly smile on the inside knowing that they are not possibly in any form of danger for me doing so!! I seldom or If ever refuse the wife when she asks me to get Icream! Also at times I will buy her one and not get anything for myself and secretly enjoy the freedom to do so without apprehension!

I seldom speak to my family or anyone about my military days and how it has affected me because I try to live in the present moment and not dwell on the past as much as I possibly can. I am constantly telling my wife to not think about the past and just live for today and be happy regardless of the bad things that happened in the past!!

This year I am starting to talk about things a little more because my old army room dog and I are going down memory lane for the first time in over 30 years. this book including all my service day's memories is intended to share some of my past in hopes to help other veterans and civilians alike face and and get through the difficult times in life we all have faced and will in our futures.

Life truly is short and my wish for everyone is to be happy and fulfilled as much as possible!

the west side of the Berlin wall near
checkPoint charlie in 1986!

West Berlin near Checkpoint Charlie

A Gift From my wife I keep on my dresser!
A Part of History that will be a Part of me
till I breath my Last!!
Love You Forever!!!

# the Purple Heart

My dad was a man of few words to the extent that he never told me that his older brother was wounded in WWII and recieved a purple heart. I only learned of this after my dad passed away and I was having a conversation with my uncles daughter about the family and she showed me his purple heart medal and the orders that had explained why he recieved it.

My family on both my parents sides have a long history of family members who have served in our nations military!!

I personaly have worked with a man who had a purple heart from vietnam and was one of the few survivors of a certian battle I will not name! Many veteran will share some of their memories with other veterans that they do not share in public!

I did have the honor of listening to a local highly decorated vietnam officer at a special ceremony in his honor when the village I live in was declared a purple heart village. He has passed away but the stories he shared with myself and a certian dignitary at this ceremony after it was over were still so alive in him that he talked as if it was like yesterday in his memories. He was not overly emotional when he spoke but I could see that the scars of war never truly heal !!!

# Annual Protest Against US

Every friday before we were dismissed for the weekend when not in the field traning we recied the do not go places alone speach by top! Some groups of people I will not speak of did not want us there at all. At times these groups would be targeting American soldiers when not in groups. Back then we did not have the modern day surveillance cameras everywhere or cell phone to capture everything so perps could be caught as easily as today.

So this being said American forces have been both hated and appreciated by those in foreign lands we have and still are serving in! What many may not realize is that even back in the 1980's we had a terrorist wath list along with photos and names of suspected terrorist. We had a visual reminder daily to be watchful of these people while off post in the local community of while traveling in Europe as a whole!

The post I was stationed at was as far as I know the property of the German government! All the maintenace was handled by them as well. Hans fwas the name of the man who was in our barracks fiting our issves as they came up. He spoke fairly good english but I tried to greet him in German when I seen him.

# Annual Protest Against US

My guess is that the army paid a good
amount of money to to rent/lease this
post and the land around it for our trainings.
   While I was there my post had a yearly
lockdown day to allow the protesters to come
to the gate and protest against us. As I
recall no military personel could come into
or leave the post for that 24 hour period of
time the protesters could be there!!
   The German Police were all over the place
outside and inside the post. Those of us on
post were on a higher alert status then
normal even though the Germany Police had
about 500 men and vehicles to take care of
the protest. I can't recall the actual distance
from the main gate to any building on post
but I will guess about 1/4 mile.
   We could venture as far as our rec center
on post but had strict orders to go no furter
or talk to any of the German Police on post.

# All humans will have Physical Pain in Life

    I am no different than anyone when it comes to having Physical Pain. To claim that I should recieve more empathetic support because I am a veteran would be very foolish on my Part. Yes I put myself through a lot Physically to be a infantry soldier and have some Painful issues later in life because of it but that was my choice to do so no extra empathy for me is required!!

    No Person will ever go through life without a good degree of Physical Pain Enough said!!!

83

# Veteran/civilian suicide

All suicide is a very tragic thing and should never be taken lightly!!

this is a difficult subject to broach but I feel it's necessary to do so. I personaly know a person who has done this horrific thing. I had a personal brief conversation with this person less than a week prior to it. It did not appear to me that this person was in that level of personal distress!! I have known this this person since I was a boy. though we were not the best of friend when we ran ~~into~~ into each other we shared a few moments of the what's up and how are things conversations.

Also a coworker of mine years ago did this also and again I hadabrief conversation with a few encouraging words in the same week that this individual took their own life. Even though I fully understand that I did not personaly cause these two the distress they were in it will not prevent the momentary thoughts of sadness when this topic is mentioned.

the old saying that it takes a community to raise children makes sense to me but also the prevention of suicide takes us all to be looking out for our fellow humans.!! Enough said !!!!

## the Bradley Fighting Vehicle

In 1986 the Army introduced us to the newest combat vehicle created for mechanized infantry called the Bradley. We all had to become qualified as a crew member of this new killing machine as I call it. the Bradley replaced the M113 personnel carrier that only had a 50 caliber machine gun as its main weapon. the bradley on the other hand has the ability to take out most any vehicle including tanks with a tow missile system even when traveling at 25 mph. the bradley has a 25 mm main gun along with a coax 7.62 machine gun and port firing weapons that covered both sides and the rear of the vehicle. It also had severl types of grenade launchers mounted on the front of the ~~turret~~ turret.

We spent 2 straight months in the field to learn and understand everything about this new killing machine. My mindset was that I needed to master everything about this vehicle so I was 100% prepared and I could also help my squad or anyone else in the company be prepared as well.

Bradley Port Firing weapons!
A fully automatic weapon used from inside.
A ventilation system along with a brass and link catching bag system was used while firing them.

Side view of a Bradley in the field

tow missile launcher

port Firing weapon

# Memories and thoughts

About the same time the bradley training was completed and we returned to post the ~~~~ Army introduced a new machine gun gun that was called the SAW - Squad automatic weapon. I being the m60 gunner was a bit hesitant to give up my 60 but after the first live fire with the SAW I loved it's capability. this was now my new baby to carry. It was I believe 17 lbs instead of the 23 lbs the m60 weighed and the ammo was the same 5.56 used by the m16.

Other than the ammo the other major difference was the Saw could send about 1 thousand rounds down range in 1 minute. It would not be a wise thing to do that but I can say from my personal experience that a 200 round belt of ammo only last 12 seconds holding the trigger down without releasing it. As a machine gunner you need to be able to have control of the volume of lead you send down range and not waste ammo.

Not that long after I had the saw I was moved to HQ to work directy for the XO and sadly had to give up my automatic weapon and leave my squad and roommate. From that point on I had no roommate!

## memories and thoughts

I did get to keep my 45 cal pistol for security duty in HQ.

My life in HQ was a lot different than in a line platoon. My line platoon leader was promoted and moved to the XO (executive officer) position and he shortly after that wanted me to be his driver and right hand man.

This officer was a West Point grad that I was asked to teach by my platoon Sgt when he first arrived to take over as our platoon leader prior to his promotion. Along with the XO I was tasked with teaching other classes to my other platoon mates. The task of teaching was not taken lightly by the CO and that was a great honor to me to be chosen to do so.

After I was working directly for the XO he did teach me a lot of things that the line guys were not privy to as line soldiers. As a matter of fact I got to be a part of some of the meetings held by the XO, CO and first Sgt. I needed to know things as the XO's driver because it was only him and I together on company missions in our M113 he was in charge of. It felt a bit crazy at first because I was only an E4 but involved with higher level information.

89

## memories and thoughts

I was made to take over as the company mail clerk as well as part of my new duties. It took a bit but I transformed my mail room into the cleanes most organized room in the company! When the Generals inspection came around he was pleased with my proficiency and organizational skills. though I knew my fellow platoon mates the best I learned and got to know everyons sevad and platoon they belonged to. Even when we were in the field we got mail call once a week. the CO gave me a bit of leeway to hand deliver mail to individuals when the company had a little down time. Remeber down time did not mean that we did not still have security measures inplace.

As hard core as I could be I still had a fun-loving side that would show up to give any fellow soldier a needed boost. Even today my hard core spirit is difficult to subdue at times and the wife gladly (Ha Ha) reminds me I am not in the army and she is ~~one~~ not one of the troops!!

From a young age I have been mostley a self-driven person and able to live and work hard without other peoples prodding or encouragment.

## Memories and thoughts

I am not a loner type but often do prefer a few minutes of solitude at times. This was evident when I refused to go out with the boys and party and stayed on post to pull extra duty or self study.

As the driver for the XO and mail clerk I did have to be self-driven because I had my own schedule other than morning formation and PT with the company. On a daily basis I got no help and was on my own. I was expected to have my M113A2 track ready for combat at all times this fully loaded vehicle had some equiptment that no other track had and I was fully responsible for it all. At times in my life it seems a bit disheartening that at 20 years old I was in charge of millions of dollars worth of equiptment and in my entire life time of working I have only earned a fraction of that!!!

In winter months all the vehicles had to be started every 12 hrs to insure we were combat ready at all times. I had hardly ever any help with this task ever on the weekends so at times I would do the entire companies vehicles when I was in HQ so the line guys could get a break. This would take about 40 min: for my track alone twice a day every day!!

91

## Memories and thoughts

The XO and I had the company's only 50 caliber machine gun which was our vehicles main weapon. The 50 cal was my favorite machine gun to fire but not so fun to carry from the armory to the motor pool hundreds of yards away because it weighed about 70 lbs I think. That was half my body weight at that time.

The CO also put me in charge of remedial PT for any rank soldier in the company that did not do well on our company runs. This was a challenge because higher ranking soldiers had to listen to me and knew I would report to the CO without question or hesitation what they could or could not do. It's a tough thing to balance respect and also demanding respect and performance from higher ranking soldier in the company you must work well with to accomplish the mission above all things.

Prior to HQ when I got promoted to the rank of specialist (E4) the Lt decided I should recieve blood rank!! An old tradition that I hope is not no longer practiced. I do not recall anyone else in my platoon ever recieving this in a promotion ceremony.

## Memories and thoughts

Blood rank is when they pin the new rank insignia to you but do not cover the pins and everyone gets to pound your rank insignia while you stand at attention and say nothing!! Probably one of the most painful things I have been trough in my life without making a sound! they say that a woman giving birth is the most painful experience a person can have but I think this ranks in very close to that level of pain! But no man will ever know truthfully because we don't go through childbirth pain

While I was in HQ I was required to do security duty for the XO because he was the Pay officer! Every Payday each month I had my loaded 45 cal pistol to guard him and the money. My recollection is that he had over 100 thousand dollars we picked up from the Post Bank to pay those in the company who had a live check to cash.

Top (First Sgt) would also use me to drive him places he needed to go. the most fun part was that we had the newest vehicle that replaced the old army jeep called the hummer. It has been a common vehicle for decades now but I like to think the military version will

# Memories and Thoughts

alway be the best. I did drive it on the autobahn and it did go up to 60 mph with the governor on.

Another of my duties in HQ I recall doing in the field was the total destruction by fire of the CEOI ( Communications-Electronic Operating Instructions) booklets when changed out. I can speak on this now because its been such a long time and this vital part of secure communication was entrusted to me. The CEOI books were the specially created communication booklets to ensure secure communication between all tracks, Leadership personel and the battalion commander as well.

Secure communication is and will always be a vital part of any military operation in times of peace or war.

Looking back I still wonder at times why I was trusted so much by the CO, XO and top to be in charge of things that are normally carried out by higher ranked soldier within the Company. Even a few years later my karate teacher asked me to teach a few classes for him when he could not be in class and I wasn't a black belt yet!

I recall one time while not on duty the XO ask me to join him in the Officers lounge.

# Memories and thoughts

I had to refuse because I was not a officer not that I didn't want to because it was a thing that could have gotten us into trouble. Officers are not to fraternize with the enlisted soldiers under their command. The XO knew I had his back no matter what but could not be seen publically as friends. though privately in his office we would have the unseen brother like bond and I learned a lot from him as well as giving him my 2 cents worth privately of course. the CO and TOP also had private conversations with me not heard by others and they taught me things the line soldiers were not privy to!!

For understanding the main reason that the officers and high ranking NCO'S are not supposed to be the best of friends with the men they must be in charge of is the fact that they must be able to make life and death decisions and put their troops in harms way. So it's best to not have close personal friendships with the men you may have to send out a may be killed in battle.

For example in WWll the top officers had to plan D Day and knowingly send thousands of troops to their death to invade and rout the Germanys in france. In modern history the former President did this aswell.

# Memories and thoughts

We all know about Seal team 6 and the mission to get Osama bin Laden and the danger they faced these type of mission happen in war or peace time within most countries world wide even those we are not friendly with.

As soldiers we had to be able to trust each other and especially with the XO and myself because we were a two person only team. As his driver I had to know and do things the line soldier did not. For example we had to be scouts for the Company and choose sites that the Company would use as temporary holding locations while on training missions. I recall the time in the middle of the night in blackout conditions leading each of the Company vehicles to their designated position the XO and I chose. As always we had to create 360° security and set basic lanes of fire for each Bradley. All the Bradlies had night vision capability but I had night vision goggles to get the job done.

When in the field most guys did not get more than 4-5 hours of sleep a day including all the officers!! I remember well the company did a night foot march to a location and it was so dark that you had to hold the ruck of the man infront of you because you could not see him!!

## Memories and thoughts

    The company did a vehicle road march to get to a training location one time and that was the hardest ever road march. The old m113 I had to drive took a good amount of effort to drive and it took 13 hours no stopping.

    The comradery in the military is like no other I have experienced in life. I do have a good level of respect for all first responders as well. I was on my local rescue squad for 5 months and training to be an EMT but was forced to quit due to painful issues with my lower back disc issues.

    When I first arrived in Germany a program existed in which a German family would host a single soldier and invite them to stay for 2 days during the Christmas Holiday. Not having any fear of of meeting complete strangers in a foreign country I signed up as soon as I learned of it. I arrived in Germany on December 9th and on the 24th I was in the Home of a German lady and her 11 year old daughter. So Christmas of 1985 at the age of 18 I was spending my first ever christmas away from home with people I had never meet till christmas eve and sleeping in their home! Another single female soldier was also their with me..!!

Memories and thoughts

thinking back that lady must have had great trust and respect for us to allow perfect strangers in her home with just herself and daughter. Out of respect I never asked about the father of this young girl or IF she was single or married. In 1986 I was back at her home for Christmas but this time I was alone!!

Many of the German people spoke enough english to understand each other in a general conversation but I had my little translater book with me to help. In 1984 this lady took me out and taught me things about her country. Also on christmas eve she had others over and we shared stories of how Christmas was in both our countries. this second year I made sure that I had a camera with me and took many photos of our time together. By the time my second year in a row that I spent Christmas with these two ladies was over I grew to appreciate them like family away from home so to speak.

Being shown that as a American others in a foreign county appreciated our mission their gave me a bit more incentive to be the best soldier I could be while serving to protect my country and theirs as well.

## Memories and thoughts

This was a valuable lesson to me at a young age to be sure not to judge people because of what ~~cout~~ country they live in but according to their individual human qualities. Bad apples live everywhere but the vast majority of people do wish to live in peace and need the same basic things in life. the freedom to make a happy life for ourselves by personal choice is a universal need I believe every human has. Unfortunately not all people are free to choose for themselves how to live and what they can do with their lives. I think about the kindness I was shown as a foreign soldier all those years ago and it gives me a more realistic hope for humanity than what can be seen on the news at times.

The two trips I took while overseas are great memories for me as well. I took a skiing trip and a trip to Amsterdam. the skiing trip was fun but because my feet still turn in slightly the tips of the of them would cross and down I went. I was downgraded to be with the kids beginners class so I wouldn't get hurt. I think it help the kids feel better seeing an adult having trouble as well and we shared a few laughs together

## Memories and thoughts

My buddies razed me good but we all had a great time. I must of not been thinking very good at the time because I did not have a camera with me. So I made sure I had one for our trip to Amsterdam.

My trip to Amsterdam was the most memerable because I got to see the house that Ann Frank hid in to avoid detection. that house was turned into a museum and it brings real perspective to the holocaust!! If the world goes unchecked this kind of atrocity could happen again.

While in Amsterdam I also took the canal tour around the city on those small Boats that held around 20 people. I still have the wooden shoes I purchased over 35 years ago as a souvenir and memory of my trip. Unfortunately 2 weeks after I got back to the States my parents had a house fire and I lost some of my favorite personal memorabilia items from the time I spent in Germany that were irreplaceable!!

I am fortunate most all my photos and paperwork survived at the bottom of my footlocker. My dress uniform got scorched but I kept it but had to get rid of the badly damaged ribbons that I have never replaced yet because serving was never about awards it's about love of country and freedom!!

## Memories and thoughts

I did recieve two awards for my military service but have never displayed or even talked about them untill I started writing this book. after Steve and I started talking about our Army days. Very few have seen them but maybe I should have a least shown them to my parents when they were still around. I have never believed in a mindset of being any form of show off so to speak! But Steve and a female friend strongly suggested to me that its ok to be proud of ones accomplishment!

We all have less than great memories as well as good ones and I did experience several in my service days. the worst is when we lost as a battalion a comrade in a training accident. the details are in my conversations with Steve.

Another guy who was a roommate before Steve and a guy I was in basic with had a bad accident as well.

During a breaching exercise he got wrapped up in concertina wire. I got myself into some trouble - vebaly that is - because I heard him let out an unforgettable scream and I immediately picked up my 60 and ran to insure the track that was wrapping him up would stop and call for the medics. It still is the most worthy ass chewing you can get because a mans life was in the balance so to speak!

# Memories and thoughts

I was also involved in a training accident and those details are also in my conversation with Steve. It took about 150-200 stitches to put my buddy back together again and a long recovery time. I don't think any human will ever go a lifetime without being involved in some form of accident that causes some degree of harm both physically and mentally. Some of life's memories can still be fairly vivid years after the events take place. As with most all humans memories can **come** up in our minds from time to time or in our dreams. From my understanding if memories old or new are still causing a negative emotional reaction after about 18 months or so we should probably seek some form of **assistance** that can reduce our painful negative reactions. PtSD can come in many forms and degrees but if it is not addressed it can lead to life altering anxiety depression and so on...!!!

Martial arts training and teaching has proven to be immeasurably helpful over my lifetime in maintaining good overal health both mentaly and physically!! Also good nutrition plays a vital role in maintaining good mental and physical health.

## Memories and thoughts

Because I still participate in martial arts training at age 56 I can still pass the push up requirements that a 20 year old soldier needed to do in order to remain qualified in the 1980's.

For the past 40 years martial arts training has had a huge impact on my life and it is hard to describe it all. I met the girl who would become my wife of almost 33 years now!! I was helping to teach a class in the late 1980's and she came into class as a student of 18 years old and the rest is history so to speak. After about one month of being in a martial arts class (traditional karate) I set a goal that some day I would be a black belt! teaching became a relentless goal of mine at the age of 16. I was a small guy at around 130 lbs when I started class and I did not have to sit the bench so to speak because in team sports only a select few are playing at once and the rest are just watching. I loved being on team sports but with karate every person got to determine their own level of participation. Each rank level had its own requirement and their was no bench to sit on while the class was going on because instruction was provided for every rank level. The workouts and drills were for All.

# Memories and Thoughts

With martial arts classes ones skill level was directly determined by the individual effort of each student and not based on what players were picked to play in a sporting game. I learned that karate and other martial arts are not just to learn fighting skills but to build individual character and physical fitness.

Similar to military comradery my class mates in class became like family and we would work hard together to grow in skill. As I think back even though I have been on my own for years now I am glad that those who were fellow black belts pushed each other in class. I will always have gratitude for the other black belts who pushed me.

Back in January of 1991 when I recieved my black belt I was made a part of the black belt board of directors within the association I was a part of. Being part of a group of my mentors was both humbling and a part of my continuing education at a higher level. I was now one of the judges at the association competitions held 3 times a year. Yes the black belts also competed and were judged by the association founder and President along with a few of the highest Level black belts under Him! Our competitions were never based on size but on rank levels.

## Memories and thoughts

Yes I did fairly well in competitions from the time I started training and throughout the years I was with the association and my teacher till I struck out on my own. I discovered that many times the most difficult people to train with and teach are family members especially the wife!

to continue to grow one must at times push yourself and students as well. I did push my wife knowing I would get some negative feedback at home. In my opinion we should never water down things that could be needed in a real confrontation. I never get bothered or upset at negative backlash because I know my students get my best as a teacher and I have taught realistic things that can help them be safer and less fearful in life itself.

For years now my mission has been to teach younger students and instruct ladies self-defence courses. I teach adults as well but my biggest pet peeve in life is the abuse in any form of children and women.

All my life I have been a believer in a higher power in a religious sense and believe in not judging others and to employ the concept of treating others in the same way I would like to be treated. But in the same breath fully believe as a veteran and martial arts teacher that evil actions must—

# Memories and thoughts

be delt with on the spot if needed even if
it requires harming a attacker in battle or on
a pesonal level to escape safely.

Evil is in my viewpoint the main reason we
humans throughout history have killed each other or
commit crimes agains our fellow man!! without
people willing to risk life and limb to keep evil
from totally taking over the world we would have
complete chaos on this planet and no form of
freedom or peace would exist.

We all have a story to tell and a childhood
dream or goals in life. I also believe that most
everyone has a few people in their lives that have
been a mentor and inspiration to them along
life's journey. As far as I see it no person has
every been succesful in anything without the aid
of others. true success is not measured by the
size of your bank account or your status in this
world. If you have a goal no matter what it is
and you work at it and achieve it thats success!!!

Never stop after a goal is achieved and I hope
that no person thinks that the goal of having a
healthy body and mind is ever achievable and works
at it till he/she breaths no more. Never stop
because of failures!! Success would not exist
without the existence of failure!!!

christmas with host family

Christmas with host family friends.

host Family

my first time ever seeing live candles on a christmas tree

My wooden shoes I got in Amsterdam.
I am so glad they were at the bottom of
my footlocker when my parents house had that fire!

My scorched uniform minus the ribbons and qualification badges I removed.

the XO and I with the 50 cal our main vehicle
weapon and me with a COAX machine gun from a Bradley!

# Boat trip

Boat trip

# Boat trip

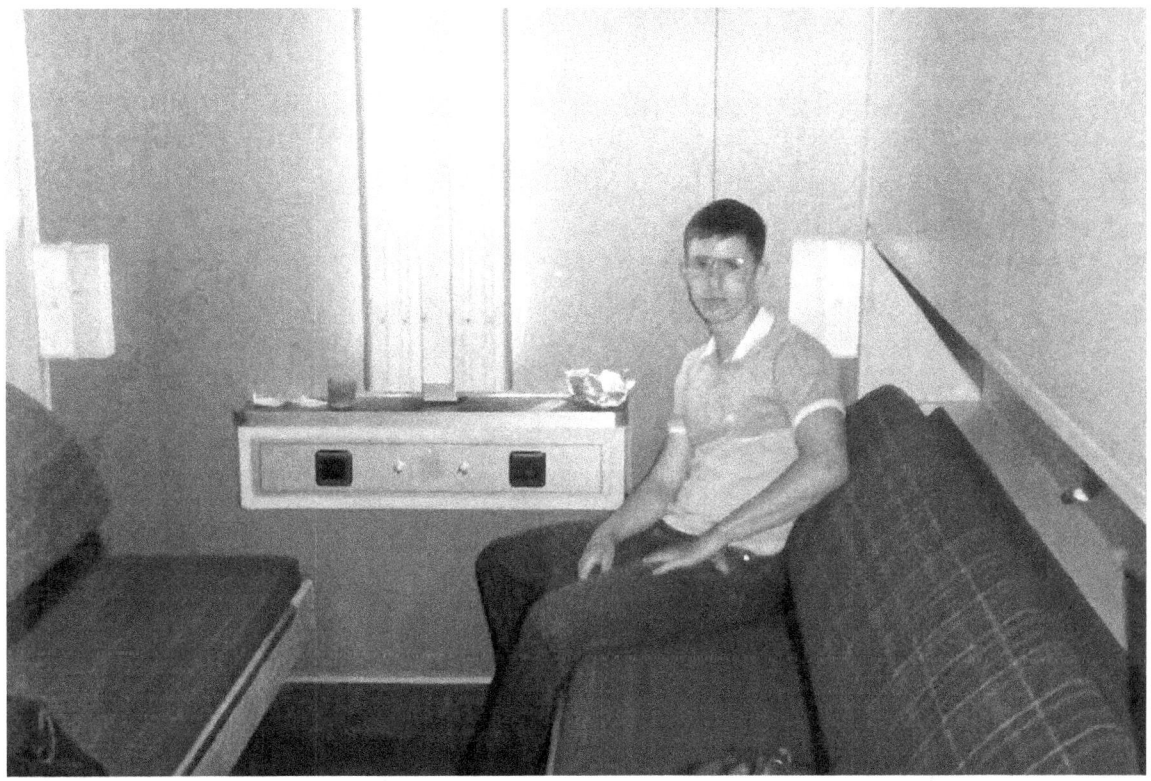

Amsterdam canal boat ride

# Bergen Belsen

My company took a trip to the site of the former Concentration camp called Bergen-Belsen. We all walked around the grounds and monuments erected for the mass graves there!! Another place in my military days I will not forget.

If you ever want to get some true perspective on how horrible it was for those people do the research but be warned that it's not something to allow young children to view in my opinon until they can handle the truth about this brutal part of history when millions of people were tragically killed!! I have seen the images and it is ~~very~~ very disturbing to see and think that humans could do such things to other humans as if they were animals.

I believe that I may have a bit more understanding of this tragic part of history because I have been able to see in person this former concentration camp and the annet/hidden rooms Anne Frank her family and others escaped detection in for about two years. My feet though fourty plus years later have walked in the same places she was and where she died. So reading her books and stories of her young life and horrific experiences touches the cord of humanity within me like no other person I have read about in my life!!!

A MASS GRAVE SITE MARKER AT BERGAN-BELSON TAKEN IN THE 1980'S. WE MUST NEVER FORGET AND PREVENT THIS TYPE OF ATROCITY FROM EVER HAPPENING AGAIN!! 5000 SOULS AT THEIR FINAL RESTING PLACE. MAY THEY REST IN PEACE!

# After the Army

I came home from the army with two main goals at that time in my young life at the age of twenty one! You can see I did achieve one of my goals by recieving my black belt but the other goal of spending about 20 more years in the national guard to be eligible for a military service pension was never realized.

I have always been a family oriented person so I spent much of my time with family outside of work and training in martial arts!! I did have the honor to help train my dad because he joined class for a good long time and started in his mid sixties! The wife and my eldest son trained also for a while with me.

My son at age five joined the kids class that I was a helping instructor of twenty five years ago!

My dad taught me the true meaning of being a humble man!! As his son he would ask me to work with him and teach him outsid of class time. He alway Ad addressed me as Sensei and would say yes Sensei when a I wodd ask him to make a correction on something that could be improved upon! A Parent who looks to his child to teach him something is in my opinion

# After the Army

the mark of a truly humble spirit!

I can learn new things from any student and often do.

As a child my family would spend a lot of time camping! My parents used their summer vacation every year to go to our local campground. My parents had a camping trailer from the time I was a child till my mom passed away in 2007.

As often as I could I took my wife and kids camping as well. In 2018 I did a full season of camping from April to September. For many years my aunt would camp seasonally with my parents in her trailer as well. A few other extended family and friends also camped for many years with us when I was a child and continued after I returned from the service.

Unlike much of this modern world where people are addicted to their technology, video games and cell phones we sat by the fire, played many games of cards and hit the campground beach!! One of my favorite memories of family gatherings is our penny poker nights. We all would save our change and showed up with a wide variety of containers full of change to play.

# After the Army

Unfortunately many family members have left this world and the camping weekends and large family gatherings are a thing of the past but the memories are for life!!

The wife and I were married on December 15, 1990 in the first good snow fall of the year! Our first born son was born on April 22, 1994 and the wife named him after me. Many unplanned things happen in life but some are verry welcome like the call I got saying I was going to be dad again. We wanted more children but were not planning for two in diapers at the same time is all. Joshua was born on November 27, 1995.

At times I swear that they planned on back to back soiled diapers as soon as I got home from work!! Nothing is more fun like having two children in diapers at the same time! Over the years my boys have learned a good amount of martial arts and at time like to attack me unexpectedly! Details of their lives is in my viewpoint not my right to speak of but I will say they are doing well. Steve did tell me it was ok for me to share our time in the military and our conversations.

121

## After the Army

I am not a big video game person but will play from time to time. the family does play non video games and such on a regular basis. when my father was alive we played cribbage all the time together.

As time has passed my family dynamic has changed a lot but the good times along with the challenges most everyone faces in life has definitely given meaning to the old saying "If your feet hit the floor in the morning it's a good day".

I may not be able to relive the days of old but do embrace the changes life brings and will continue to bring as I have gotten older.

Life will always move forward in time but lasting memories that go back to our childhood through the present will forever be creating the person we are today with every passing year!!!

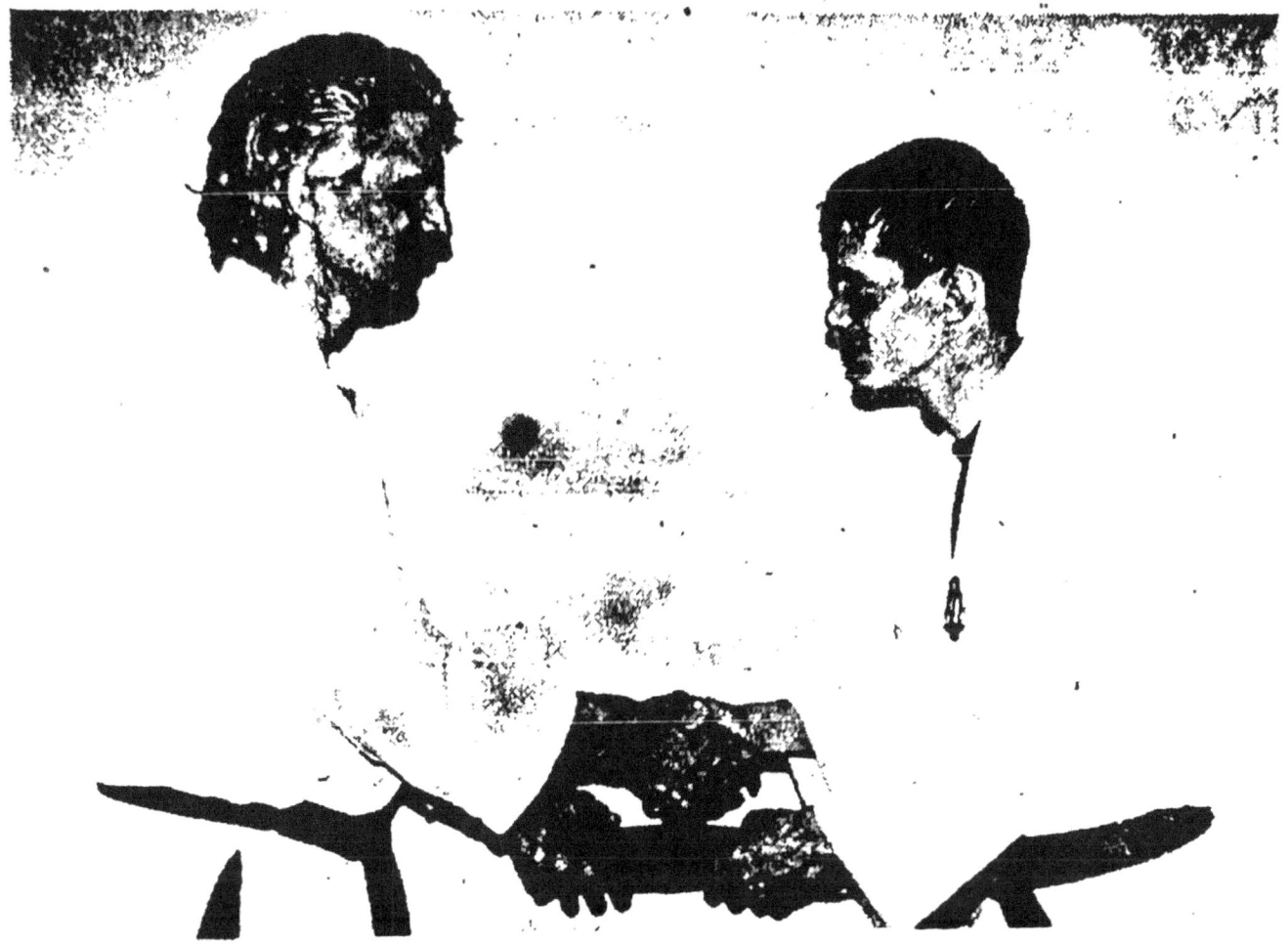

Alan Haskell receiving Black Belt from Instructor Martin Davis. ❏

# Alan Haskell receives rank of Black Belt

Alan Haskell, son of Clarence and Pearl Haskell of Shushan, NY was recently promoted to the rank of Shodan - First Degree Black Belt by the Cambridge Branch of the Triangle School of Karate.

Alan began his training with the Triangle School of Karate when he was a junior in high school in Hoosick Falls. He trained for nearly two years and then served for three years in the Armed Forces. After his term in the service he again continued his training with the Triangle School of Karate and upon completing his requirements was promoted by his instructor, Martin Davis and the Board of Black Belts, to the highly admired rank of Black Belt.

Present for his promotion was honored guest, Master Louis Stanishia, president of the Triangle Karate Association, headquarters in Yorktown Heights, NY.

Alan, the sixth one from the Cambridge Branch to reach Black Belt, has also placed several times in the past in competitions of Kata (forms) and Sparring in Yorktown, including 1st place in Kata in January of this year.

His instructor and fellow students, which include Alan's father, are proud of him and feel he has a superb attitude and the desire to always be the "best he can be." ❏

**TRIANGLE KARATE ASSOCIATION**
**SANKAKU KYOKAI**

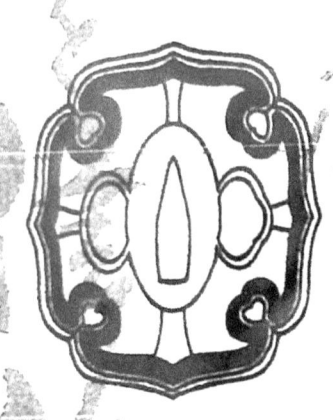

空手道

AWARDED TO

**Alan Haskell**

ON THIS 26th DAY OF January 1991,

AFTER HAVING COMPLETED THE PRESCRIBED

REQUIREMENTS OF THIS ASSOCIATION,

ITS ANCIENT FORMS AND DECORUMS,

THE RANK OF Shodan, Black Belt.

*Martin E. Harris*

SENSEI

*Lou Stanishia*

SHEEHAN
President, Sankaku Kyokai

124

# 4TH BATTALION

## 41ST INFANTRY

### 2ND ARMORED DIVISION (FWD)

UNITED STATES ARMY, EUROPE and SEVENTH ARMY

# CERTIFICATE of ACHIEVEMENT

## IS AWARDED TO

SPECIALIST ALAN B. HASKELL,

For outstanding performance of duty while assigned as driver for the Executive Officer of B Company during Bradley gunnery training at Bergen, FRG from 6 November to 21 November 1987. With very little supervision, SP4 Haskell kept his track in a high state of combat readiness. Keeping an aged and ailing M113A2 in top running order in a field environment is a demanding and difficult task. However, SP4 Haskell's solid sense of responsibility and devotion to mission accomplishment enabled him to keep his vehicle and equipment mission capable. SP4 Haskell's outstanding performance of duty reflects great "FIX BAYONETS" credit upon himself, the "Fix Bayonet" Battalion and the United States Army.

**THIS** 7th **DAY of** January **19** 88

William

WILLIAM T. VOSSLER
LTC, IN
Commanding

125

# 2d Armored Division (FWD)

**HELL ON WHEELS**

## United States Army, Europe, and Seventh Army

This

# Scroll of Appreciation

is awarded to

SP4 ALAN B. HASKELL

For

OUTSTANDING DUTY PERFORMANCE AND EXHIBITION OF PROFESSIONAL SOLDIER CHARACTERISTICS DURING YOUR TOUR OF SERVICE WITH 2D ARMORED DIVISION (FWD), LUCIUS D. CLAY KASERNE, GARLSTEDT, FEDERAL REPUBLIC OF GERMANY. THIS SCROLL OF APPRECIATION IS PRESENTED AS TESTIMONY OF YOUR EXCEPTIONALLY DEVOTED SERVICE TO YOUR UNIT AND TO ATTEST TO THIS COMMAND'S APPRECIATION FOR YOUR DEDICATED PERFORMANCE. THE ARMY THANKS YOU FOR YOUR PROFESSIONALISM, COMPETENCE, AND CONTRIBUTIONS IN THE DEFENSE OF OUR COUNTRY.

TOMMY A. BAUCUM
Colonel, Armor
Commander, 3d Brigade

This ___29th___ Day of ___April___ 19 ___88___

Form 253, 1 Oct 84

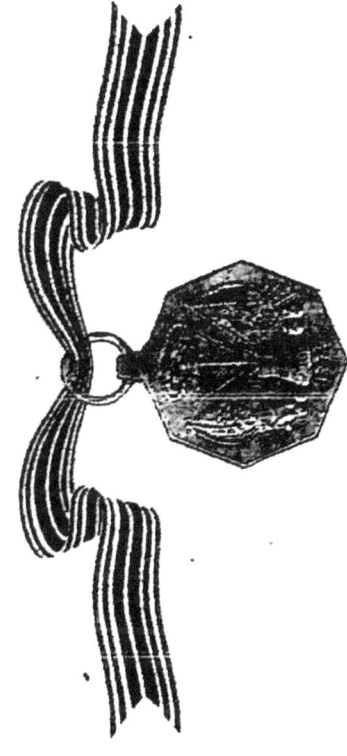

# DEPARTMENT OF THE ARMY

THIS IS TO CERTIFY THAT THE SECRETARY OF THE ARMY HAS AWARDED

## THE ARMY ACHIEVEMENT MEDAL

TO      SPECIALIST ALAN B. HASKELL, ▃▃▃▃

FOR exceptionally meritorious service while serving with B Company, 4th Battalion, 41st Infantry from 9 December 1985 to 19 May 1988. SP4 Haskell performed duties as Assistant M60 Gunner, M60 Gunner, M113A2 Driver and Company Mail Clerk. His aggressiveness and eagerness to learn have made him an inspirational and able soldier. During Bradley Transition, he scored 100% on all tasks tested. His ability to perform without supervision earned him the position as M113 Driver for the Company XO. During the 1987 Annual General Inspection, his mail room received laudatory comments from inspectors. SP4 Haskell's outstanding performance is in keeping with the finest traditions of the military service and reflects distinct credit upon himself, the "Fix Bayonets" Battalion and the United States Army.

GIVEN UNDER MY HAND IN THE CITY OF WASHINGTON

THIS   19th    DAY OF    May    1988

SECRETARY OF THE ARMY

WILLIAM T. VOSSLER
LTC, IN
Commanding

127

# Honorable Discharge

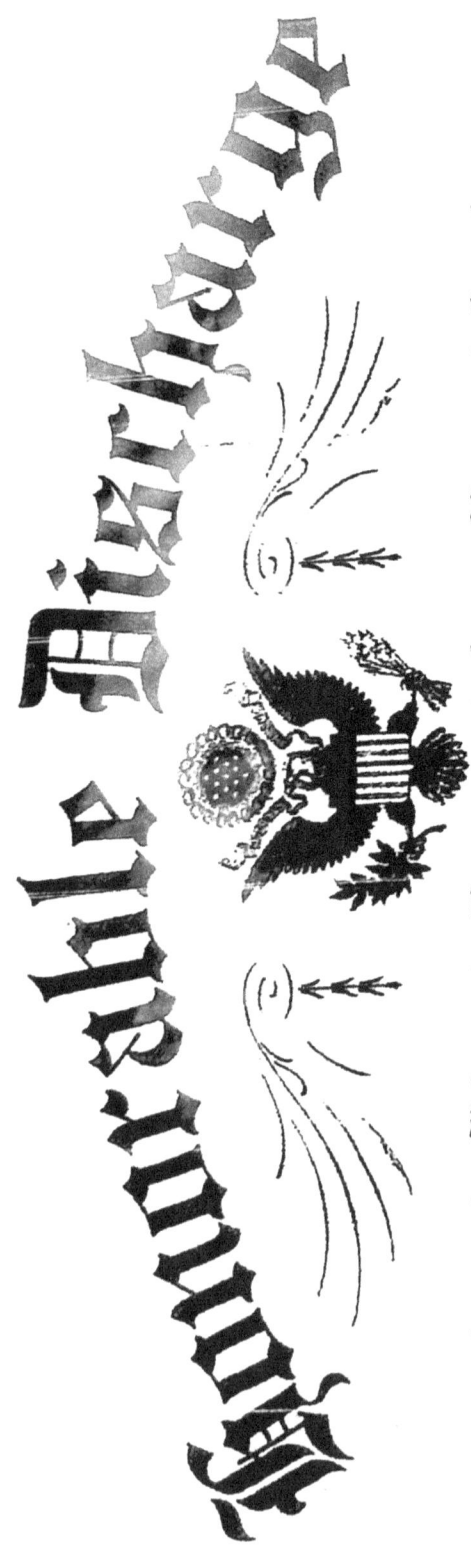

from the Federally Recognized Army National Guard

*This is to certify that*

ALAN BURTON HASKELL  SERGEANT CO C (-) 1 BN 210 ARMOR

*was Honorably Discharged from the*

# Army National Guard

of  NEW YORK

*on the* 14th *day of* NOVEMBER 1991  *This certificate is awarded*

*as a testimonial of Honest and Faithful Service*

"This discharge does not relieve the individual named herein from any unfulfilled obligation to perform military service which may be imposed on him/her by law."

CHARLES M. AMOROSO, CW3, NYARNG
Assistant Adjutant General

128

# A note about
## Veterans & Civilian Suicide

It is extremely difficult to know what the mind of an individual has going on as far as self value/worth and personal self talk is concerned!

Are we feeling that we no longer have purpose and value to others? Are we feeling we are a burden to others especially family and friends ? Are we feeling unusable or unnecessary to others in the way we once were or felt we were? Has my purpose or participation been so diminished that I am a waste of time and space in the eyes of others!! Do I matter at all anymore?

Do these thoughts come on a daily basis or just in a rare fleeting moment that passes without lasting impact? The reality in my mind is we all have had these types of thoughts at some point in life to one degree or another! I know I did in my youth and at moments even to this day!

The challenge is to be able to, without fear, share those thoughts and feelings with another person! Most will share and display them on a surface level as in yelling at others or other detrimental actions, but rarely ever speak the exact thoughts on their minds!

I have done it and  has put me in the line of fire several times even though what I have said was truthful and my authentic thoughts! The scrutiny we get for sharing authentic, truthful information we are thinking can lead to outcomes that are not always good!

Oftentimes it's the people we care about the most that can say or do something that hurts us the most in life because we tend to share more of our truthful innermost thoughts with them! The outward signs of a person on the pathway to attempting suicide may never be clear to those around that individual!

When thoughts of taking one's own life are revealed, the recipient of any form of that inclination must not brush it off due to the fact that they are reaching out for help in many cases!! If nobody has any form of reaction or response this could possibly lead to a more serious matter and possibly the act of attempting suicide!! Not all but unfortunately too many first attempts at suicide are successful!!!!

If we have previous knowledge of an individual's conditions like depression, anxiety, and such I feel we must take some form of action to help! If we don't know what to say or do just not leaving this person alone is a form of intervention after this type of speech is heard! Then communication with those people who are also around this individual is imperative to let them know this type of thinking is happening, in my viewpoint of course! We tend to spend most of our time around co-workers, family, and friends but could possibly notice some of the signs of a person in distress!

The more educated and aware of the signs of what could be someone having deep internal distress and thinking or acting in a careless suicidal way, the better we can prevent a person from following through with life-ending actions! Unfortunately we have seen way too many who hurt or kill others then take their own life after or want someone else to kill them in the process of committing a violent crime!

How many times have people knowingly taken drugs and have overdosed intentionally, or not, and by intervention are saved? This is possibly higher in number than we are aware of and that's a harsh reality of the world we live in today! If we all watch our family and friends closely and act to prevent suicide as a human race we can reduce this tragic thing called suicide!

I have heard a high ranking military officer say that many people who are feeling lonely on the inside and never talk about it can be a driving factor in suicidal thoughts and behaviors! Yes I do believe this is accurate because I myself have felt a bit lonely at moments in my life after I got home from the service! Feeling lonely is not because we don't have people in our lives! We can be surrounded by family and friends and still feel nobody understands us and the feelings we have!!

I hope the conversation of feeling alone or misunderstood can be opened up a lot better for all of us!

All my life I have had the drive to be helpful to others. Since joining the military at 18, teaching has been my passion in life. The best part for me about teaching the martial arts I started learning over 40 years ago has been watching students progress in their physical abilities while also seeing them develop good characteristics of a martial artist. They learn tools for self protection, and life as a whole, as the also get in touch with their mind, body, and spirit. I am currently the comander of the American Legion Post I am a member of. Learning and sharing is a life long pursuit of mine.

Alan Haskell
Army 1985-1988
Army National Guard 1988-1991